Buckminster Fuller

Buckminster Fuller

MARTIN   PAWLEY

WITH PHOTOGRAPHS FROM THE BUCKMINSTER FULLER INSTITUTE

TAPLINGER PUBLISHING COMPANY, NEW YORK

First published in the United States in 1990 by
Taplinger Publishing Co., Inc.,
New York, New York

ISBN 0 8008 1116 X

Design by Elizabeth van Amerongen
Cover design by the Armelle Press
Manufactured in the United Kingdom
For more information concerning Buckminster Fuller
please contact the Buckminster Fuller Institute, 1743
South La Cienega Blvd., Los Angeles, California 90035.
Phone (213) 837 7710

contents

acknowledgments

As the bibliography of this book indicates, *Fuller* is only one of a large number of books written with and about Richard Buckminster Fuller, in addition to magazine special issues, articles, features and transcribed speeches over the last 50 years, most of which are based on a deeper personal knowledge of the subject. With the exception of one encounter that is described here, I lacked this advantage and so *Fuller* is a book based on secondary sources. In this respect, like all writers on Fuller, I owe a profound debt to three predecessors: Robert Marks, whose *Dymaxion World of Buckminster Fuller* opened mine, as well as many other students' eyes thirty years ago; John McHale, whose *R. Buckminster Fuller* has rested on my bookshelves for almost as long, and James Meller, whose *The Buckminster Fuller Reader* first showed me how rewarding Fuller's own difficult writing could be. I must also mention Lloyd Steven Sieden's extraordinarily detailed *Buckminster Fuller's Universe: an appreciation* which I have leaned on heavily, particularly for my account of the demise of the 'Wichita' house project in 1946.

Last but not least, this book would have been impossible to research or illustrate without the generous and friendly help of John Ferry, Janet Brown and Michael Hines of the Buckminster Fuller Institute, Los Angeles, California.

to connect the support of the fifty men robbed of their work by machines to the productive capabilities of the robot. By perpetually extending the mechanical man in the direction of the human economy, the designers of the 20th century created a world that had never before existed in history. They found ways to close the interface between human consciousness and the man-made material world. Where once technology killed, now it fits. Where once the machine was feared, now it is embraced - and both transformations were carried out by design.

That the designers of the 20th century really have connected the necessity of support with the abundance of invention is a proposition that requires little proof. Even the most extravagant interpretation of human needs in 1933 could scarcely have included one tenth of the goods and services whose universal distribution has today been rendered normal by the activity of design. The multifarious inanimate energy slaves of the late 20th century city would have struck the employer of 1933 as a nightmare of implied social support. Fifty robots instead of one! Who could support the 2,500 men thus thrown out of work? Nor would the answer to this question have seemed credible: that tasks would be created that sixty years ago did not exist. These new tasks, and the purchasing power they have created, are the engines that power the expanding universe of design and production today. The symbiotic phenomenon of design and economic life now exists at a level far beyond the wildest dreams of the industrialists of sixty years ago. Design now sustains economic activity. Already, sixty years after that *Punch* cartoon, design has become the key to the new material world that can support fifty times fifty men. Design is the interdenominational networking of form that makes sense of consumption. From the ten-speed racer to the VCR to the cellular telephone to the workstation to the communications satellite, design is the adhesive that binds all to the global economy. In the end it is design that makes the buying and selling of information as intelligible as once was the buying and selling of slaves and cotton.

But if the new role of design as the engine of consumption is as evolutionarily important as this, how are we to understand its individual workings? At the level of production economics, designers seem no more than a human sub-species, like bees, who work without character or individuality. Indeed today, in investment terms, it has become possible to see the whole design profession in this way, but this is a very recent development.

'Design Heroes' is a series about the individuals who shaped this now homogeneous world of post-industrial design. Men and women who did not resemble the stereotype of today's designers, but who nonetheless created their world of present possibilities for them. Although they seldom worked entirely alone, these 'Design Heroes' established themselves as individual talents, rather than as members of packs like today's design consultancies; packs that are identified by strings of names, cryptic initials or acronyms. These interchangeable box-suited ray-ban figures driving BMWs may be quoted on the USM or listed on Stock Exchanges all over the world, but they are not 'Design Heroes', yet. The classification is reserved for those bold individuals who staked out the first claims in the virgin territory that the corporate designer of today is content to methodically comb and recomb.

Who were these prime individuals, the creators of a new genre of creative human being? The question is more difficult to answer than it might appear, not least because it is only in the last few years that the synergetic importance of design and economics has been popularly grasped.

In the 20th century design always existed, but for years it was not recognised as an unitary phenomenon and its practitioners did their work under different titles with different degrees of status. Sometimes what we would call designers today were 'chief draughtsmen', sometimes 'engineers', sometimes 'inventors', sometimes 'craftsmen', sometimes 'artists', sometimes 'amateur con-

9

structors'. In fact the best of them were always Heroes if, consciously or unconsciously, they worked to the dictum of Nietzsche: 'Need is not the reason for something to come into existence, it is an effect of what has already come to be'.

This series of short biographies is an attempt to tell, through the lives of a number of great 20th century designers, how the question posed by the *Punch* cartoon was, and is, being answered. The 'Design Heroes' are men and women who somehow and in some way overdrew on the bank of invention, and in doing so revealed something of the inner mechanism of the creative individual under stress and thus helped to define the elusive modern term 'designer'. All these individuals have been chosen because, in widely different ways, their lives and their works deliver the essence of design as a vital human activity.

We know that it was determination, stamina, endurance beyond the call of reason that created the 'Heroes' of exploration; the 'Heroes' of warfare; the 'Heroes' of speed and flight. design too makes its calls upon determination, stamina and endurance. 'Design Heroes', like all heroes, are individuals who have been beyond the point of reasonable withdrawal. They have suffered for their work and their convictions. They have overstepped the bounds of conventional behaviour in order not to relinquish the creative integrity of their work.

We know from history that it was not science, but design that created the first engines to pump water; the first mechanical tools to lift rock, bore tunnels and bridge rivers; the first ships that could sail against the wind. Design too created the man-made environment and defined the limits of the dreams of what might still be possible within it. 'Design Heroes' is not a series about the great inventors of the 19th century. It is about the generation that grew up with the elements of the modern world, the car, the passenger aeroplane, the spacecraft and the computer. Men like Richard Buckminster Fuller, whose long life encompassed the history of flight and the history of prefabrication. Raymond Loewy, who designed railway locomotives as well as the interiors of NASA spacecraft. Harley Earle, the creator of the surrealistic finned monsters of the post-World War Two American automobile industry. Ettore Sottsass, who worked on the first Olivetti computers before he broke free from the constraints of Modernism altogether and entered a revolutionary new creative world of furniture design. Colin Chapman, who founded a high-performance automobile legend that he used every resource, even forbidden ones, to keep out of the hands of corporate predators until he died. Tom Karen, who turned a three-wheeled van and a defunct sports car prototype into a hatch-back driven by Royalty.

Through the lives and works of designers like these, the series 'Design Heroes' will change our understanding of what those men and women did who truly learned how to make more production out of less work - by design.

Martin Pawley
Series Editor

introduction

'Making the world's available resources serve one hundred per cent of an exploding population can only be accomplished by a boldly accelerated design revolution to increase the present performance per unit of invested resources. This is a task for radical technical innovators, not political voodoo-men.'

Richard Buckminster Fuller 1970

Although he was never an architect, the work and ideas of Richard Buckminster Fuller found an audience in the architectural profession for most of his life. This association began unpropitiously in 1928 with the American Institute of Architects' unceremonious rejection of the gift of the patent rights in his revolutionary '4-D' prefabricated house. For a time it continued as a love-hate relationship, with Fuller occasionally painfully sarcastic in his dispraise, as in this 1966 gem from the American magazine *Architectural Forum*; 'The architect is a slave; the client says 'I am going to build a building on that corner; this what the building codes and labor unions say you have to do; I want my relative's materials used, and my wife wants it to look like this.' And it ended 50 years later in reconciliation, following the award of uncounted honorary architectural degrees, professional fellowships, medals and titles, and an almost legendary status amongst architects and architectural students all over the world. A tireless public speaker, in the year of his death at the age of 88 Fuller twice circumnavigated the globe, lecturing to packed campus audiences in universities and schools of architecture.

Born of patrician New England parents, Fuller broke a tradition of more than century by failing to graduate from Harvard university. In later life he attributed what technical training he possessed to his service as a junior officer in the US Navy during and after the Great War. Following that conflict he worked for many years in the construction industry, gaining bitter experience of the limitations governing the machine production of building materials and their public acceptance at that time. Like many others he dreamed of emulating the automotive and aviation achievements of Henry Ford, first by producing a revolutionary car called the 'Dymaxion' - DYnamic + MAXimum + IONs - and later by applying the methods of the automobile and aircraft industries to the production of housing.

Fuller was the first pioneer of prefabricated housing to understand that cost-effectiveness in this field depended entirely on a drastic reduction in the weight of the product. His 1929 project for a steel, duralumin and plastic 'Dymaxion House' was for years illustrated in newspapers and magazines as the prototype for the mass-production dwelling of the future. An early variant was even proposed as a lightweight, multi-storey apartment tower for air-delivery anywhere in the world by Zeppelin.

In World War Two Fuller's expertise in the field of lightweight demountable housing was enlisted by the US government. It led not only to the construction of thousands of steel 'Dymaxion Deployment Units' (emergency USAAF aircrew accommodation modified from steel grain bins), but eventually to the famous 1946 'Wichita' house, a full-size family dwelling weighing only 4 tonnes that was designed to be assembled on wartime bomber production lines. The prototype 'Wichita' is the most important prefabricated house design of the 20th century, and certainly the greatest lost opportunity of the years of post-war building recovery.

These early failures are dealt with in some detail in this book as part of an effort to combine the usefulness of a short biography with a critical evaluation of Fuller's best known inventions and theories, from the 'Dymaxion House' to the concept of ephemeralization. An additional function that they serve is to shed some light on the long psychological battle that Fuller's own fertile and boundless imagination enabled him to fight against failure and critical rejection.

Fuller's only great commercial success, and his best known invention was the geodesic dome, a triangulated space-enclosing technology that was domical in shape in order to enclose the maximum internal volume with the minimum structure. Patented in 1954 no less than 300,000 Geodesic Domes were built over the next 30 years, for purposes ranging from sports arenas to subtropical housing and the construction of a permanent American base at the South Pole. Projected dome structures included mile-diameter flying spheres and floating cities. The last in a long line of Fuller's dome refinements, the revolutionary 'Fly's eye dome', also intended as a cheap dwelling enclosure, was still under development two years before his death.

But despite this last great victory, for most of his life Fuller remained not only outside the mainstream of American industrial production, but outside the mainstream of accepted design culture. His revolutionary 'Dymaxion Car' - unique in being rear engined but front-wheel driven, and intended to speed along roads like a taxiing aeroplane - was toyed with by the United States motor industry for more than a decade, but its ideas were never taken up in the form in which he introduced them. His even earlier predictions of the feasibility of 'jet-stilt' air-cushion vehicles played no part in the subsequent development of the helicopter or the hovercraft.

As well as being a futuristic and prophetic designer, Buckminster Fuller was author, co-author, or a major contributor to over 50 books, and the subject of thousands of newspaper articles and interviews. In all of them he proselytized tirelessly for the creation of a world design science to avert ecological catastrophe and promote resource conservation, notions that were a generation ahead of their time.

Today, less than a decade after his death, Fuller's reputation is poised uneasily between oblivion and cult status. It fits somewhere between the heaped honours of an architectural profession that has already largely forgotten him, and a growing environmentalist opposition to all uncontrolled industrial production. This balance is so delicate that, while ecologists and environmentalists in their new Green political prominence could do no better than to seek a framework for their ideas in the collected works of Buckminster Fuller; the withdrawing forces of industry too - under attack from every quarter for exhausting resources and polluting the environment - would also find a 'blueprint for survival' in those same pages of ideas and inventions.

For the master of 'more for less', if he were still alive, there might be something gratifying in this pregnant symmetry.

'Goldylox and the Airplane': a portrait of Fuller drawn by his wife Anne Hewlett Fuller in 1928.

brief encounters

'I asked myself, '(1) Can you trust yourself never to turn to your own exclusive advantage the insights entrusted to you only by the realization of benefits for all humanity and the Universe itself? (2) Can you also be sure that you will never exploit your insight by publicly declaring yourself to be a special 'son of God' or a divinely ordained mystic leader? (3) Can you trust yourself to remember that you qualified for this functioning only because you were an out and out throwaway? (4) Can you trust yourself to reliably report these facts to others when they applaud you for the success of the experiment with which you were entrusted?'

Fortunately, I can, may, and do report to you that I have never broken that trust nor have I ever been tempted to do so.'

Richard Buckminster Fuller 1983

Over the years of his life, thousands of writers and journalists interviewed Buckminster Fuller. There is no record of all the interviews he gave. A 'Basic Biography' published by the Buckminster Fuller Institute in March 1983 reproduced the titles contained in the cuttings file of the *New York Times* from 1922 to 1982, and revealed 520 items. Assuming that only one quarter of them involved interviews of one kind or another, and taking into account perhaps another 50 major newspapers and magazines world wide, we can see that Richard Buckminster Fuller might have been interviewed 5,000 times.

Among the last of these countless interviews was one carried out by Fuller's admirer Dr Anwar Dil, the co-writer of the book *Humans in Universe* published in the year of Fuller's death. As a document Dil's interview is long and predictable for the most part, but suddenly, in the midst of an exhaustive discussion of what the sage's final message to the parents and children of the world should be, Fuller says - and in the light of the statistics given above we can be sure that he is telling the truth - 'Everything I have said to you, I have written or said before.'

'Would you at this point make a statement that you have not written before? What would that be?' Says Dil.

Fuller thinks. Then he replies; 'One of the things that interests me is something strange that occurs on every occasion of my making a scientific and socially advantageous discovery and a special-case technological invention therefrom, in general support of my attempting to solve human problems with technology.'

'Whatever the discovery and invention may be, I have always had the experience of some enchanting female coming into my life concurrently with the scientific discovery. You, Anwar, have brought my darling wife into our discussion. despite flirtations and sex with others, I have never stopped loving my wife above all others. What I am getting at here is the Iliad and the Odyssey or Aeneid like sirens or other females' interceptions of the explorer's route. This has repeated itself a number of times in my life. Every time I am about to make a discovery and I am developing a high sensitivity of thinking, along comes a, to me, exceptionally charming female with whom I find myself tending to fall in love. Only when I have successfully restrained myself from falling further and have applied myself exclusively to the discovery or inventing, and only then, do the critically relevant conceptions occur which secure my comprehension of the significance of the discovering and/or inventing and what my responsibilities are in making the discovery and inventions effectively available to humanity.'

'At any rate, that is something I have never written before. I suspect it may be importantly true.' Unlike

Anwar Dil, I only ever had one face to face encounter with Richard Buckminster Fuller. It took place thirteen years before the occasion on which I last heard him lecture, ten days before his death, when he spoke at the Royal Institute of British Architects in London on the occasion of the award of the Royal Gold Medal for Architecture to his former collaborator and friend Norman Foster. Foster was, at that time, designing a complex double geodesic home for Fuller that was to have been erected on a site in Los Angeles. On the earlier occasion thirteen years before, I had been sent to interview Buckminster Fuller for one of the first issues of the magazine *Building Design* . Prior to that encounter I had only an abstract impression of him, formed by seeing his name and his projects, chiefly domes, in books and magazines. The idea of his role and personality that I had gathered was negative. Fuller, I believed, was a kind of mathematical huckster, in some suspicious way connected with American foreign policy. He was, I thought, a dangerous technocrat, trying to remove the subjective, creative element from architecture and replace it by universally applicable geometrical formulae. Notorious for lecturing student audiences for four and five hours at a time, Fuller seemed to me to be a heartless, totalitarian figure, crucially lacking in human values.

Years before the interview that was to transform my perception of the man, I had put this unfounded prejudice in writing. In the early 1960s I was a member of a dissident student group at the Oxford School of Architecture called the 'Progressive Architecture Movement' which had leafleted the audience at a British Architectural Student Association (BASA) conference addressed by Fuller. The leaflets, which I had composed, bore (to my eternal shame) a suitably modified picture of the sage's head with the slogan; 'Come off it BASA! Buckminster Fuller's head is a geodesic dome. Inside it is a copy of the *Reader's Digest* '.

So grandly are the paradoxes of life arranged that twenty years later it was an excellent article about Buckminster Fuller by Emily and Per Ola d'Aulaire in that very magazine that confirmed my desire to study the story of his life and write this book.

On February 28th 1970, the day that I interviewed him, Richard Buckminster Fuller, then aged 75, was staying at the Stafford Hotel in St James' Place, London, a quiet cul de sac near Piccadilly. With him during the interview was Shoji Sadao, his longtime Japanese collaborator who is today curator of the Isamu Noguchi gallery in New York. Fuller and Sadao were in England to discuss the proposed, but later abandoned, Samuel Beckett Theatre in Oxford. This project was to have been carried out in association with an admirer of his, that same later RIBA Gold Medallist, the architect Norman Foster.

My plan for the interview was simple. Filled with the overweening confidence and scepticism of youth I was determined to show Richard Buckminster Fuller and the readers of *Building Design* that I for one would not be put off by two hours of autopilot geometrical and algebraic nonsense about the universe like all the other Fuller groupies. I wanted to make Buckminster Fuller talk about the housing problem (a subject I believed that I knew something about) and not about domes or icosahedrons. The next two hours were not a success from the standpoint of this plan.

For a start Fuller was late for our two o'clock appointment. I and the staff photographer had to watch horse racing in the television lounge for ten minutes before he and Sadao arrived at the hotel and led me up to his small room on the fifth floor. Once there Fuller ordered a fruit salad and a pot of tea from room service and we all sat down. At 75 he was stiff of movement and clearly hard of hearing, but his energy was surprising - as when he sprang up to open doors, pulled up chairs and indulged in elaborate mimicry to make a point. I later learned that he had been taught these athletic movements, as well as his extravagant lecturing mannerisms, by his daughter, the dancer Allegra Buckminster Fuller.

After the photographer had left, I moved in with my first question. It was a killer. 'Mr Buckminster Fuller, forty-three years ago you announced that a world housing industry using advanced technology was inevitable, yet every one of your efforts to bring such an industry into existence, before, during and after the Second World War has been a total failure. Why do you suppose that is?'

Fuller's astronaut-stubbled head stared at me with what looked like unseeing eyes through pebble glasses whose frames incorporated stereo hearing aids. His whole body, reshaped by his stiff suit, collar and tie as are those of most thin old men, was immobile, his brain working like a computer sorting something out. 'I would contradict that completely', he replied evenly. 'In the first place because no world housing service industry can ever be based on products that people can buy. It is a whole process. If people had to go to a market to buy all their own guts, with them hanging up all around, nobody would buy them at all. There's not any part of a human being that anyone would buy if they did not already have it anyway'.

I felt myself losing the initiative. This reply was tangential but not perhaps totally irrelevant. I temporized.

'What about brains. Wouldn't they buy brains?'

'What those awful things!' Fuller laughed. He had figured me out. 'OK, so that's where you start'.

From then on he went on to explain what he meant by a process instead of a product, using the story of how the telephone system had been successful precisely because the instruments had never been sold, only rented. In the interests of recording a minor comment on the present state of the telephone industry it is worth noting that he predicted exactly what has happened now that telephones are sold. 'If they ever sell telephones', he said in 1970, 'before long you will get a Christopher Wren telephone, a Louis XIV telephone, a World War One trench-type telephone, then an alligator telephone... All this horrible equipment you will pay a terrible price for and it will stop development of the service itself'. Then he resumed his narrative.

'The lesson of the telephone taught me back in 1927 that housing was going to have to be a service industry, not a product industry. A truly logical complement to life embodying the principles of nature, recogniz-

'Notorious for lecturing student audiences for four and five hours at a time,' Buckminster Fuller at Black Mountain College, North Carolina in 1948 with the prototype Venetian blind dome *(left)*. Seven years later an audience of English scientists who worked on the Cambridge DNA/RNA discoveries *(below left)* endures a Fuller lecture on synergy.
Fuller the explorer *(below)* in a kayak off his family's · later his own · summer home on Bear Island, Maine in 1911; Fuller the sailor *(right)*, at the wheel of the family boat *Wego*, volunteered for United States Navy patrol duty at the entry of America into the Great War. Fuller the talker *(below right)* holding forth in New York in 1947.

ing entropy and the inevitability of change. A bird picking up twigs to make a nest turns the whole action into a complement of its life. A spider makes a web, a mole makes a tunnel. They alter their environment in preferred ways. Human beings do that too. They are not unusual in that, only the extent to which they do it'.

'I say that housing has to be a service. It should be. When you use your house and think about it as we do today, as a castle full of treasure, to say; 'You're supposed to die! You stay outside my walls!' He rose suddenly to his feet with a menacing gesture - 'I can roar like a lion!' - and then sat down again and lapsed into a short, ruminative silence. Then he looked up. 'By this time you are supposed to be scared to death. Housing as an advertisement for how great you are is not what I am talking about at all'.

'Yes, but housing policy...' I interjected. Fuller waved his hand, he was coming to that.

'Now I said earlier that I would contradict you completely and I will. After the First World War I was horrified by the progress of the automobile industry in America. There were 125 car companies in 1919, but between then and 1926 they were reduced to eight companies. It was the most immoral thing I ever saw, all those automobile companies going bust, and yet it was the most successful period in automobile development - the price of Ford cars dropped by 30 per cent. That such a success should have been accompanied by bankruptcy after bankruptcy seemed to me to mean that our society just didn't understand proper accounting. I looked into it and found that the accounting system we were using was invented solely for agriculture. That was because it was the main business of man for centuries'.

'Now crops are an annual thing. Either they come in or they don't. So you get annual accounting in agriculture because it makes sense. But I realized that the gestation rates of industrial undertakings were not annual like agriculture, even though everybody was investing in them as though they were. If a productive industry had a bad year, all its stocks went down and so on. I saw that we were not thinking in the right bracket and I understood that that had accounted for the bankruptcies. It was then that I started trying to work out the *real* gestation rates for different industries taking this basic failure into account. Would it be a thousand years before man's productive thinking could be catalyzed in a better way? In which case nothing I could do would have much effect at all. Or would the timescale be much shorter?'

'Well, by cataloguing all the known inventions and scientific events, logging the rate at which scrap metal came back on the market as a raw material, I found that in electronics - then a very new industry, an invisible world in which you couldn't see the waves and they were handled mathematically so that you could prove them mathematically without too much argument - things happened quite fast. The gestation lag between invention and use in electronics was about two years. I found in the airplane industry there was a five year lag. In the automobile industry the lag was ten years. Railroading about fifteen years. Skyscraper building, a much different technology from housing, had about a twenty-five year lag. In the housebuilding business the lag was between forty and fifty years'.

'Much as I was interested in developing a new housing concept as a young man, I knew then that I had to count on half a century between intention and industrial production. If I wasn't ready to wait forty or fifty years... Don't tackle it. I knew in 1927, 1928 that anything I did during those fifty years would be premature for production, and I was right. But since that time everything has been coming in on schedule and the industrialized dwelling will be coming in too, right on the nose, between 1972 and 1975, and the new industrialized houses will look an awful lot like the Dymaxion House too'.

This was an impressive theory, but I was still prepared to stick to my guns. 'Surely', I ventured, 'there is less sign of an industrialized housing industry now than there was twenty years ago. Today we have a crisis in housing...'

'If we have a crisis in housing it is because old style housing is just about stopping', he replied quickly. 'It is in the United States anyway. In 1927 I wrote a book pointing out how the government was getting involved in housing because private industry had dropped it - not just because it was unprofitable, but because it was completely obsolete. Since that time our government and yours have got involved deeper and deeper. In the United States they have had to take over all the mortgages. We have been underwriting obsolescence for forty years. We have been trying to revive a dead man! We have got a corpse on our hands and it's taken nearly fifty years for anyone to realize that it's dead!'

Buckminster Fuller paused dramatically. His voice in the small room had risen to a boom not far short of lecturing strength. His fruit salad was unfinished, his tea undrunk, and mine too. Whenever I interjected, he seemed to get more angry: but if I did not interrupt him there was no telling where all this might lead.

'But I'm concerned about all the political changes...' I tried again.

'And I'm concerned that you started off by calling me a failure', he thundered back. 'Failure is a word invented by men, there is no such thing as a failure in nature. Man's confidence in his judgement has failed, nature never fails. Don't talk to me about failure, it's a word like pollution invented by ignorant men. There is no such thing as pollution. Nature invented beautiful chemistry and men have pulled out some here and left in some there... All we do when we pollute is make recovery and recycling difficult by spraying the waste products from one process into the air or the sea where it's difficult to get them back again, that's all. All the young people are going wild today because they know the old people have been asleep at the switch! The whole housing mess we're in comes from the ignorance and fear of financiers. The governments of the world have had fifty years to prepare for a HOUSING SERVICE INDUSTRY and they have done nothing at all!'

A thunderous silence fell across the room. Sadao sat silent at a small table. I sat in my chair. Fuller was standing, striding, limping slightly about the pathetically little space left in the hotel room.

'But don't we lose something important if we lose the idea of possession and ownership,' I tried finally, 'These things are ancient traditions...'

'You never did own a thing so you can't lose a thing', he growled in reply. 'You're losing a stupid notion that's all. You don't own anything or anybody. You don't have to own the ocean to have a boat. You don't have to own the sky to have an airplane. You won't have to own anything to have a really good dwelling service around our universe. My revolution is to make the old thing obsolete, not to attack it. The old method of housing will soon be too expensive, too slow, too cumbersome. Land ownership will go the same way, it will become a liability. These things are already happening. In the United States people buy house with loans every forty years and then leave town every four years. They buy cars over three years, and then trade them in as soon as they own them. Ownership is already out of date. Ownership is absolutely fallacious'.

Transcribing these words twenty years later, I can still feel their force, but now I can understand it better. I had thought myself daring to call Buckminster Fuller a failure, but in fact my performance had been a flea bite alongside the travelling hornet's nest of detractors of whom I knew nothing who had been saying the same of him for twice as long as I had been alive.

In later years, when I learned more of his life, I think I came to understand what being called a failure must have meant for him. Richard Buckminster Fuller had suffered mocking, cowardly, inadequate commentators stretching back before the day I was born to the very physical failure that would have pre-empted all failures for any lesser man. For he was a small and inadequate child born to a proud New England family that traced its ancestry back eighteen generations to Thomas Fuller of London, born in 1420.

When he grew to manhood Richard Buckminster Fuller was only five foot two inches tall, his head was unnaturally large and his left leg more than an inch shorter than his right, giving him a gait 'like a penguin'.

Other portraits: Fuller the lone genius *(left)* in a Greenwich Village studio in 1929 with a frame model of his '4-D' mast-supported house; Fuller the ambassador *(right)* guiding HRH Princess Margaret and Lord Snowdon around a 1962 exhibition of his work at the United States Embassy, London; Fuller the philosopher *(below)* in 1967 surrounded by geodesic models in his study at the University of Southern Illinois.

As a child he was cross-eyed, unpopular, badly behaved and bullied at school. He was sent down from Harvard, where every male Fuller since 1760 had graduated. He was bankrupted in business, where his father had been a model of probity. He was fired from jobs and ridiculed by his peers in engineering, architecture and construction. In 1927 he was sacked from his post as president of 'Stockade Building Systems' after five years. In the same year he was shattered when his three year-old invalid daughter died in his arms and her last words were; 'Did you get me the cane, Daddy?' - a reference to the walking cane he had promised to buy her when he had left the house to go to a collegiate football game – and had unfortunately forgotten.

One year later he offered the patent rights in his revolutionary '4-D' house to the council of the American Institute of Architects, whose then vice-president was his father-in-law, and the Institute not only rejected the gift but caused the gratuitous insult; 'Be it resolved that the American Institute of Architects establishes itself on record as inherently opposed to any such peas-in-a-pod-like reproducible designs', to be read into the minutes of the meeting held to discuss the matter.

At least twice Buckminster Fuller's failures were so notorious as to lead to his being pilloried by the press: in 1934 when an accident with his revolutionary Dymaxion car resulted in an outcry over the death of the driver; and again in 1946 when his prefabricated housing company 'Fuller Houses Inc' - for which thousands of dollars worth of stock had been sold on production targets of 20,000 units a year, and upon which the job prospects of 20,000 wartime aircraft workers depended - was liquidated through his own stubbornness.

The Richard Buckminster Fuller of that day in the Stafford Hotel knew what failure was, he had been called a failure by experts. In fact, although I did not know it, his success, his reputation, his immortality rested upon a structure of failures so vast and ambitious that only a man of superhuman courage and determination could have supported it.

This much I did not realize at the time, but I did understand that the end of my interview with Richard Buckminster Fuller had arrived. I had asked only one of the ten questions I had prepared, but the emotional intensity in the hotel room was too powerful for me to speak, and for Fuller, further elaboration of what he had already said would clearly have been superfluous.

As I put my tape recorder and notebook away and put on my coat. Buckminster Fuller addressed me in a different tone that showed that his anger had either been simulated, or had quickly abated. 'I hit you hard that time because I want you to remember what I said. I'm an old man and I won't be around forever'.

I shook hands with Fuller and with Sadao, who had said nothing throughout the interview, and I left the hotel. I went back to my flat in Paddington and began to transcribe the key parts of the tape. The published version was necessarily incomplete, but the essence of the encounter was there. The only important omission was Fuller's message to me as I left.

As an interview subject, especially towards the end of his life, Fuller was for the most part, as he confessed to Dil eleven years later, 'saying all the things that he had said or written before'. And today I know that the verbal counter attack, the practiced rage, and the final gruff conciliation that he employed to such effect on me - like the theatrical gestures taught him by his daughter - had all been used before.

The significance of his remark to Dil about women is less clear, it might be completely innocent, or it might represent a chink in the armour of a private man who would normally only speak of his private life as a historical thing. There were women whose names occur in the long story of Buckminster Fuller's career; Romany Marie, who kept the bar he frequented in New York City in the 1930s; Cynthia Lacey, generally described as his personal assistant, whose face makes an enigmatic appearance in most of the magazine stories about the Wichita House; Katherine Dunham, the black dancer who played such an important part in raising community support for the Saint Louis 'Old Man River' project. But outside his family and his associates little or nothing is known about them or their relationship with Richard Buckminster Fuller.

In the beginning, as at the end of his adult life, there was only really Anne Hewlett Fuller, his wife. The permanence and unknowableness of their relationship is attested in a million ways, but one of them is accessible. In the Buckminster Fuller archive in Los Angeles there is a scraperboard drawing of the polymath, seated with pen in hand at a desk. On the back of it is an inscription that reads; 'Buckminster Fuller by Anne Hewlett Fuller, his wife, sketched in their Belmont Harbour, Chicago apartment in 1928 as he completed the manuscript of '4-D', and the invention of the Dymaxion House, as an objectification of his philosophy of industrialization'. On the front, in the margin is written enigmatically; 'GOLDYLOX AND THE AIRPLANE'.

Fuller the immortal, alongside a bust of himself cast by his friend the sculptor Isamu Noguchi.

the year of silence

'Picture on the shores a city of 4-D design, in place of the hit and miss, American Institute of Bow & Arrow Boys pile-em-up, paste-em-together architecture. This 'aesthetically' interior-decorated architecture, or archaic style designing, is similar to our childhood toy shop boat-makers' products, which enrage the senses of any child who knows boats... The aesthetic drivel with which architects, who are responsible for the styles, have been educated is partly responsible for this...'

Richard Buckminster Fuller 1928

Richard Buckminster Fuller never wrote or talked about his private life except, as his former associate Don Richter put it, 'as a historical thing'. In a strangely depersonalised way he discussed the evolution of his own mind as though it were alone in the universe and still in the process of formation by events stretching back to the beginning of time. Fuller reminisced for interviewers and told his life story over and over again until it grew too long and involved to tell to anybody at one sitting, but it had only one truly personal episode. That episode was a catastrophe called 'The silent year' that came to an end at exactly the time Anne Hewlett Fuller, his wife, drew his portrait and wrote the words that we can all, almost understand.

Anne Hewlett was one of ten daughters of a New York architect named James Monroe Hewlett who had studied under Pierre Galant in the external ateliers of the Ecole des Beaux-Arts in Paris. During his life Hewlett became vice-president of the American Institute of Architects and designed the decorations for all the New York military parades at the end of the Great War. Born in 1896, Anne herself studied at the New York School of Applied Design from 1914 to 1915 and became engaged to Buckminster Fuller in July 1916. From then on she devoted her life to his support. They had two children, Alexandra, who was born five days after her parents marriage in 1917, and Allegra who was born ten years later at the beginning of the silent year. After 66 years of married life Anne Hewlett Fuller died in hospital in Los Angeles in July 1983 six weeks after major surgery for cancer. Her husband had collapsed and died in the same hospital at her bedside only 36 hours earlier.

Richard Buckminster Fuller Jr. was born on the 7th of December 1895 in Milton, Massachusetts, in a house built by his father to the design of the architect son

The house where Richard Buckminster Fuller was born in Milton, Massachusetts, now a suburb of Boston. The house was designed for Fuller's father by the architect son of the poet Henry Wadsworth Longfellow.

of Henry Wadsworth Longfellow the poet. He was the only son of Richard Buckminster Fuller, a leather and tea merchant with offices in Boston who died in 1910. His grandfather, Arthur Buckminster Fuller, was a hero. In 1862, during the American Civil War, despite his age and non-combatant status as chaplain to his regiment, he seized a rifle and volunteered to lead a charge across a bridge of boats at Fredericksburg, in the course of which he was shot dead. Arthur Buckminster Fuller's sister, and Richard Buckminster Fuller's grand aunt, was the feminist writer and personality Margaret Fuller, the author of *Woman in the Nineteenth Century*, who has herself been described as 'the greatest woman of the 19th century' by admiring modern feminists. Another grand-relative, James Monroe Sanderson, was the first manager of the Langham Hotel in Portland Place, London. Long before, Buckminster Fuller's great, great, great grandfather, the Reverend Timothy Fuller (Harvard Class of 1760), was a Massachusetts delegate to the federal Constitutional Assembly that created the United States of America.

At the time of his marriage the bearer of this intimidating lineage was an officer in the United States Navy serving in anti-submarine patrol boats off the New England coast. In his short life he had already been sent down twice from Harvard and packed off to Canada to work in a cotton mill. He had then worked in eighteen different branch houses of the Armour & Co meat packing company. In April 1917, at the age of 21, he had enlisted for the duration of the war and had prospered in the service, rising to be aide to Vice Admiral Albert Gleaves, commander of the cruiser and transport force of the United States Atlantic Fleet, charged with securing the supply lines to the American Expeditionary Force in France. In 1919 he was discharged with the rank of Lieutenant and rejoined the Armour Company in New York as assistant transport manager, in which post he remained for two years until he left to become sales manager to the Kelly-Springfield Trucking Company, which promptly went bankrupt. Fuller then returned to the Navy as a temporary reservist and was given command of the patrol boat *Eagle*. In the autumn of 1922 this short-term duty ended and he left the Navy for the last time. Very shortly afterwards his daughter died tragically of influenza.

The death of his four-year-old daughter in his own arms affected Fuller deeply. For months he remained unemployed, an unofficial pensioner of the Hewlett family. He developed an obsession with the role of old and damp housing in the influenza epidemic that continued to sweep the country. Eventually he went to work for his father in law as president of a company formed to promote the 'Stockade Building System', a method of building walls out of cement and compressed wood shavings.

Ambitiously Hewlett and Fuller opened five factories from New Jersey to Illinois for the manufacture of 'Stockade' blocks. As chief salesman Fuller spent long periods of time on the road and, according to his own account, developed into a heavy drinker. After three years he moved to Chicago in order to supervise the opening of another 'Stockade' factory in Joliet, Illinois, and in 1926 Anne joined him there. Throughout his time promoting the 'Stockade Building System' Fuller found himself opposed by sceptical architects, building control officers, contractors and competitors. Often his profit margin on a job was entirely erased by the need to put on full-scale fire tests of 'Stockade blocks' because officials would not accept the results of tests already carried out in other localities. The entire building establishment seemed to him to be one gigantic conspiracy in restraint of trade dedicated to preventing any improvement in the standard of construction.

Despite these difficulties Fuller continued to expand his operations until, early in 1927 Hewlett became pressed for money and sold his controlling shareholding in 'Stockade' to the Celotex Corporation. Fuller, as president, soon found himself in conflict with the new management. In the summer of 1927 he was forced to resign with little to show for his years of work. In August, before he had found a new job, his second daughter, Allegra, was born.

The collapse of 'Stockade' marked one of the lowest

A wall of 'Stockade' compressed wood-shaving building blocks after forty years.

points in Buckminster Fuller's life. It marked the beginning of the silent year. Long afterwards Fuller would describe the way in which he tramped the shores of Lake Michigan in despair, intent on throwing himself in once he could convince himself that his life insurance policies would be of more value to his family than he was. In the end he failed to convince himself of this, experiencing instead what he called his 'private vision'. 'You do not have the right to eliminate yourself', it advised him. 'You do not belong to you. You belong to the universe.' At the age of 32 he started out on a new life.

Moving from the expensive rented house he had occupied as president of 'Stockade', Fuller took his family to what he described as a slum, the apartment at Belmont Harbor where Anne was to draw his portrait. For the next year he refused to speak to anyone, even her. Instead he went into what can only be described as a creative breakdown, devouring books and legal pads, reading, writing and drawing with a compulsive and self-destructive energy.

Throughout this inner struggle he consumed books and magazine devoted to mathematics, science and architecture wherever he could find them. He conceived the idea of the *Graf Zeppelin*, the giant German dirigible, as 'no more than a new kind of skyscraper laid upon its side'. He noted the German project by

37

the brothers Rasch for mast-hung apartments diagonally braced to the ground like ship's masts. Like the engineers of the small but influential 'Technocracy' movement he came to believe that the United States should be run as a machine, with its currency based on units of energy instead of money. Aided by a patchwork of such ideas, Fuller pitted his recollections of the advanced, and advancing, technology he had glimpsed in the Navy against the conventional Malthusian and Darwinian wisdom that seemed to endorse war, destruction and poverty by natural example. In the end he concluded that human inventive ingenuity could be pitted against the exhaustion of resources and the injustice of poverty to produce more by design than existed in nature. Thus mankind could succeed instead of failing. Adherence to the old economy of scarcity was in fact just another conspiracy in restraint of trade, this time by financiers and businessmen determined to make the new 'more for less' technology maximize profits instead of benefit humanity.

During the silent year he devised the title '4-D' for the inventions that he scribbled down to reverse this negative balance. '4-D' stood for 'four-dimensional thinking' - thinking in time instead of only in space, thinking of consequences for humanity instead of only immediate personal gain.

Emerging at length from his furious silence he resolved to promote the artifacts of this new thinking by setting aside any further idea of commercial gain and concentrating instead on the development of a 'design science' to obtain maximum human advantage from the minimum use of energy and materials. Almost his first practical step was to endeavour to patent the design of a '4-D' mass-production house.

'Dymaxion' is the name generally given to the projects with which Buckminster Fuller emerged from his year of isolation, but in fact the word came later and '4-D' coexisted with it for many years. The word 'Dymaxion' was invented by the public relations department of the Marshall Field department store in Chicago in 1929. It was allegedly devised by listening to him talk and noting down the words that he most

Students and teachers at Milton Preparatory School, Milton, Massachusetts, where Fuller was a pupil from 1900 until 1904. This photograph was taken in his final year. Fuller is standing with the third bicycle from the right. *(Below)*, Fuller, Allegra and Anne in Lincoln Park, Chicago, in 1928 - the end of the year of silence.

frequently used - 'dynamic', 'maximum' and 'ions'. Fuller liked the name 'Dymaxion' and particularly liked the 'scientific' way in which it had been discovered. For the next five years it joined '4-D' in the name of the company Fuller formed to develop his inventions and was to be used as a prefix for all his projects for the next 15 years. He even designed a 'Dymaxion' logo which was based on a flying fish.

The biggest barriers to a proper evaluation of the Dymaxion projects that emerged from Buckminster Fuller's time of silence, apart from the congested writing of the seminal text '4-D', which is discussed in the last chapter, is the bewildering number of different stages of development in which the projects have been illustrated ever since.

'*4-D*' itself was a sparsely illustrated pamphlet that was altered and expanded for its subsequent 1970 reprint as '*4-D Timelock*', so it is unclear whether all the projects bound into the subsequent printing were in fact included in the original. But even from the latter modified printing we can taste the authentic Manifesto flavour. '*4-D Timelock*' is a rambling yet condensed document, with hasty sketches, bold chapter headings and short chapters, and frequent references to hundreds of pages 'left out for clarity' while space apparently remains for endless inconsequential correspondence from relatives and celebrities along the lines of; 'Dear Mr Buckminster Fuller, I am sorry to say I could not make head or tail of your book'.

The first '*4-D*' was in effect a transcript of the half-mad verbal Fuller who burst upon the world in 1928, talking for 16 hours at a stretch. Whether or not it contained a full inventory of the Dymaxion projects is perhaps less important than the fact that the major ones are all now world famous. What can be drawn from it is that after the silent year Fuller emerged a different man. No longer a gregarious travelling businessman, patiently expanding a market for low-cost building blocks, he has become a dynamic theorist, possessed of a seething framework of ideas that he was not to relinquish for the rest of his life.

Historically the best known of these ideas is the

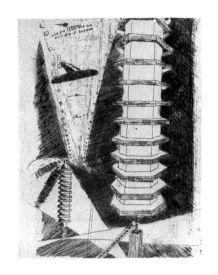

Fuller became obsessed with the capability of airships during the year of silence. He saw their light but enormously strong tensile tubular construction *(left)* as 'no more than a new kind of skyscraper laid upon its side'. Fuller's own airship-based '4-D' towers were crudely illustrated at first. His drawing 'Entering a 4-D city on the night air way express' *(right)* shows stacked apartment towers, with cranes and searchlights on their roofs, lining an airport runway. Fuller believed that giant dirigibles like the *Graf Zeppelin* could transport multi-storey '4-D' towers all over the world. One drawing *(below)* showed the installation of an airship-transported '4-D' tower at the North Pole.

unique combination of functionalism and prefabrication that is enshrined in the familiar image of a mast-supported structure called the Dymaxion House. Next perhaps are the sketches and models of multistorey '4-D' or 'Dymaxion' towers composed of 'Dymaxion houses' stacked up to ten or twelve storeys tall. Then there comes the implausible 'Dymaxion Auto-Airplane, with its inflatable wings. Later these were to be joined by the 'Dymaxion bathroom', the 'Mechanical Wing' and the converted grain bin-based house called 'DDU', or Dymaxion Deployment Unit. Finally there is the last structure in the series which is no longer called Dymaxion, although it was originally christened 'Dymaxion II'. It is the prototype house for mass production long since renamed 'Wichita' after the place in which it was built.

The dates usually assigned to these projects and structures run from 1927 to 1946. The date given for the Dymaxion House is invariably 1927, the same year as the date given to the multistorey '4-D' towers, which are clearly multiples of the former. The first Dymaxion car was built in 1933, and the 'DDU' is variously dated between 1940 and 1944. The 'Wichita' house is dated 1944-1946 but the one completed example was assembled from components in 1945.

Accurately dating these projects is difficult, and not only because all their titles are simultaneously those of sketches, drawings, projects, realized prototypes and mass produced articles. For example 1927 is not only the date assigned to the 'Dymaxion' house, but also to the first sketches of the '4-D Auto-Airplane', the forerunner of the 'Dymaxion' car, as well as the various multi-decked, mast-hung, air deliverable '4-D' apartment towers and their derivatives, the double-'4-D' tower; the double-helix parking tower, and the suspension wheel office building - all of which are also sometimes described as precursors of the 'Dymaxion' house. In the same unsatisfactory way a curiously 'mediaeval' drawing exists, also attributed to 1927, that shows the Dymaxion house to scale in elevation, isometric and plan. Even more confusingly there are plaster models of various designs for the '4-D Auto-Airplane' executed

The outpouring of '4-D' inventions from the year of silence was not confined to airship-derived towers. Fuller also sketched a gigantic 100 storey office building whose floors were suspended from the spokes of giant wheel. He also indicated a 'Double 4-D' twin-tower office building (below).

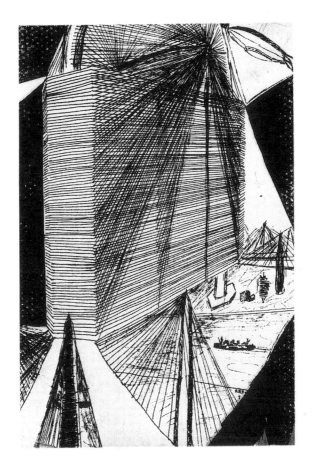

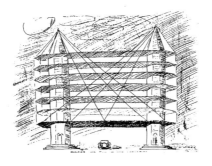

by Fuller's friend, the sculptor Isamu Noguchi between 1929 and 1932, which are often seen in photographs beneath models of the 'Dymaxion' house. Finally there is the patent application for the '4-D' house, dated 1928, that definitely appears in the pages of '4-D' but bears only a very limited resemblance to any of the other dwelling drawings or models. Common sense and what we know of Buckminster Fuller's life and his 1927 breakdown tells us that the first manifestations of the 'Dymaxion' series must be the sketches of the world of the future that first appeared in 1929 and may or may not have been included in the hand-bound edition of '4-D' which Fuller circulated privately in 1928 - principally (and fruitlessly) to bewildered relatives and such notables as Jacob Astor, Bertrand Russell and Henry Ford.

These sketches are simple and almost childish in form, except in their jagged urgency and their consistent use of unusual perspective viewpoints. They show multi-floored apartment towers being carried by airships to distant parts of the globe; rows of the same towers lining aircraft runways, with cranes atop them to raise aircraft to their roofs, and searchlights and wireless antennae prominently displayed. There are also sketches of the interiors of these towers and various derivatives of the same tensile frame structures - two-mast, cycle wheel and so on.

It is true to say that, apart from their information content, these sketches are executed with remarkably little skill. The lettering accompanying them is poor: so poor that it alone would serve as proof that Fuller never received formal architectural training. Some of them bear the initials 'RBF' and some are dated '1928'. One is called '4-D Chicago Home Exposition 1929'. Only one of these drawings, despite the chronology now sanctified by time, is clearly dated 1927. It does not show a Dymaxion house, but is a rough sketch of the world seen from space, with aircraft flying between '4-D' towers located on all continents including the Arctic and the Antarctic. At the bottom of the drawing is the rubric '$=TIME' and an hourglass.

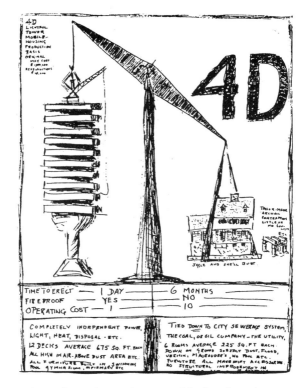

Apart from date written on this drawing, the year 1927 is only retrospectively found in Fuller's publications, as for example in the captions to the well known photo-series showing the erection of a Dymaxion House model featured in *Fifty Years of the Design Science Revolution and the World Game*. This document was published 40 years after the event. It was in fact 'prepared for free distribution at the joint national meeting of the Operational Research Society and American Astronautical Society, Denver, Colorado, 17-21 June 1969'.

There is no evidence that the designs for what Fuller called the 'clean-up' version of the 'Dymaxion' single family house existed before 1929, when a detailed model of it appeared alongside a display of modern furniture in the Marshall Field department store in

Chicago - for the first time under the title 'Dymaxion' instead of '4-D'. Nor is there evidence that any of the sketches of the '4-D world' existed before the 'publication' of '4-D' itself. Finally there is no proof that any scale drawing of the 'clean-up' version of the 'Dymaxion' house existed before the unusual 'mediaeval' drawing with its patterned lettering that, according to Robert Marks, was published by the Harvard Society for Contemporary Art in May 1929.

These may seem to be picayune discrepancies to draw attention to in a short account of Buckminster Fuller's life, but there are deeper uncertainties beneath them, particularly when the '4-D' patent application house of 1928 is introduced into the picture. For there is a shattering contrast between the '4-D' house shown in the US Patent Application made by Fuller on April 1st 1928, and the 'clean-up' or '1927 Dymaxion house' that has been portrayed in drawing, model and mock-up ever since.

Unlike the 'clean-up' Dymaxion, the '4-D' patent house is seldom illustrated. Its appearance is utterly different even though its construction is technically similar in that both are based on a single tubular mast with tension-supported floors. Structurally the most important difference is that the '4-D' patent application house is rectangular in plan, while the 'clean-up' Dymaxion is hexagonal, so that all its spans are equal.

Externally the '4-D' patent house is grotesque, betraying once again its designer's lack of formal architectural training, but in an entirely different way to the lettering that accompanies the published '4-D' sketches. Where the lettering on the sketches is crude, the elevation of the '4-D' house is artless. Its pyramidal metal roof and metal walls are punctuated by enormous windows subdivided into small panes, and the doors, front and back, are both revolving - for reasons connected with the operation of the air conditioning and ventilation system. According to the patent application, internally the house was to have pneumatic rubber floors laid over corrugated steel decking. Its external walls were to be formed from suspended sheet metal screens, and its internal partitions from inflatable curtains; 'not unlike the body protector worn by a base-ball catcher'. The decoration of these partitions was described in surprising detail; 'one side might be a light blue tapestry suitable for a bedroom, and the other side might be a white waterproof oilcloth or linoleum suitable for a bathroom'.

All writers about Fuller in the past have been either too cursory or too partisan to address the important questions raised by the discrepancies between this '4-D' patent application design and what subsequently became known as the 'Dymaxion' house. Most fundamentally none has ever asked whether it might have been this '4-D' design that was offered to the American Institute of Architects as a gift in May 1928, and not the futuristic 'clean-up' version immortalized by photographs of the model in the Marshall Field exhibition. On the contrary. Most assume that the Marshall Field version of the 'Dymaxion' house was patented. It was not. Nor in fact was the '4-D' house. The patent application of April 1st 1928 was rejected and, although Fuller could have pursued the matter like any other applicant, he elected not to.

Given the length and complexity of the full patent application, and the time and effort that would have been involved in producing another one and another set of drawings in time, it is almost certain that it was the archaic-looking rejected '4-D' patent application of April 1st 1928 that Fuller magnanimously offered 'full proprietary rights in' to the AIA one month later, and not the 'clean-up' Marshall Field version that appeared in the following year. This judgement is confirmed rather than denied by the evasive treatment of the question in Buckminster Fuller's own book *Inventions: the patented works of R. Buckminster Fuller*. In this book, published in the year of his death, Fuller shows some drawings and text from the patent application, but intermingled with photographs of the quite different Marshall Field model, with no explanatory distinction between the two.

Somehow Fuller transformed the artless 1928 patent application design into the elegant 'clean-up' model. How and when he did it is a mystery that is intensi-

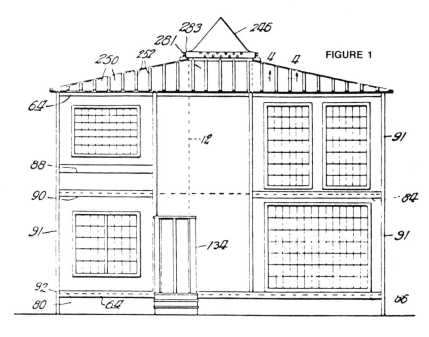

FIGURE 1

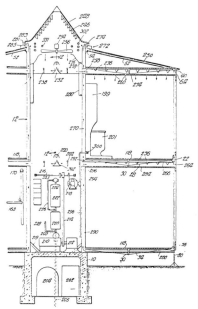

The dramatic evolution of the Dymaxion House. April 1928 patent application *(left)* shows a primitive rectangular metal dwelling with revolving doors and crude elevations. Only section *(below, left)* shows family resemblance to later Dymaxion. This was the house design notoriously rejected by the American Institute of Architects as a 'peas-in-a-pod' approach. The first drawing of the 'clean-up' version *(right)* which has since become world famous, appeared in this curiously 'mediaeval' form in May 1929.

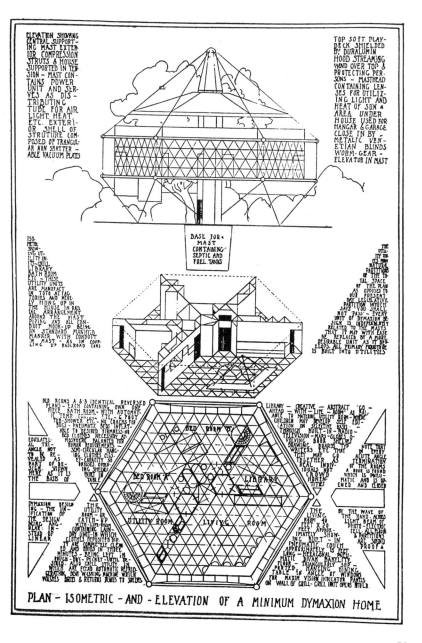

PLAN - ISOMETRIC - AND - ELEVATION OF A MINIMUM DYMAXION HOME

fied by the '1927' date generally assigned to the sketches of '4-D towers' that look more like the 'Dymaxion' house than the apparently later patent application. Here is a feat as miraculous as the transformation of the bizarre and impractical 'jet stilt', inflatable-wing '*4-D Auto-Airplane*' into the first road-going 'Dymaxion' car.

In fact the 'Dymaxion' house transformation is even more miraculous than the 'Auto-Airplane' metamorphosis because, in the latter case, we know that another individual was involved. He was the well-known aircraft and yacht designer Starling Burgess, who Fuller first met in a hotel in New York City in August 1932 and talked to for four and one half hours. Burgess was a key figure in the genesis of the Dymaxion car. He developed Fuller's analogies between the shapes and steering mechanisms of boats and fish and motor vehicles, and he knew as much as anyone in the world at that time about streamlining and tension structures. Burgess not only designed seaplanes, but three Americas Cup defenders, including the 1930 victor *Enterprise*, with its revolutionary $50,000 duralumin mast and perforated duralumin boom, a triangulated rig that saved over one ton in weight over the steel used by the British challenger.

It is a matter of record that, after their meeting, Burgess went to work with Fuller at the '4-D Dymaxion Company' in Bridgeport, Connecticut, where the Dymaxion cars were built. It is also recorded, by Fuller himself, that Burgess calculated the dimensions of the central mast for the superimposed floors of the proposed ten-storey Dymaxion skyscraper, and Burgess who designed the aerodynamic screen that enclosed it. But this was not until 1932. The assistance of Burgess in a similar but earlier transformation of the '4-D' patent application dwelling into the now famous 'clean-up' version of the Dymaxion house can probably be ruled out on chronology alone.

There are of course other possibilities. Fuller's father-in-law, James Monroe Hewlett, might have exercised a benevolently intended but unfortunate influence over the preparation of the 1928 '4-D' patent application and attempted to render its appearance more conventional. Hewlett had, after all, jointly with Fuller, already filed one patent application - for the 'Stockade' building system that was granted in 1927. Alternatively the 'clean-up' model may have started out as an unclad structural model of the patent application house. Or perhaps another figure, possibly the unnamed 'wordsmith' who invented the term 'Dymaxion' at the behest of the Marshall Field publicity department, played a part. 'Dynamic', 'Maximum' and 'Ions' are all we know about this man, but anyone who could invent a term like 'Dymaxion' must have been extraordinarily capable.

Whatever the explanation for this minor mystery, it is a fact that the first publication of the 'clean-up' version of the Dymaxion house in a professional architectural journal was not in 1928 or 1929, but three years later in 1932, in the March edition of *Architectural Forum*. Two months later it appeared in the May 1932 edition of the magazine *Shelter* with Fuller's own Corbusier-style collection of design influences for the

Dymaxion house: lighthouses, water tanks, even a piggery. Six months later Fuller's ten-storey 'Dymaxion' skyscraper with its aerodynamic cowling - radically different to the 1928 '*4-D*' sketches as a result of Burgess's structural and streamlining skills - makes its first appearance in the November 1932 edition of *Shelter*.

However the '4-D' metamorphosis was carried out, its results were immediate and beneficial. From the 'clean-up' version onwards several models of the 'Dymaxion' house were constructed for exhibition and Fuller began to lecture on the subject of a world prefabricated housing industry using '*4-D*' or 'Dymaxion' designs.

Later improvements to the originally crude and unstable '4-D towers' followed the progress of the Dymaxion house. 1930 Chicago drawings *(below)* show suspended floors and triangulated central mast. 1932 Starling Burgess version shows tapered duralumin yacht spar construction with more convincing and broader based shrouds, as well as transparent aerodynamic shield to reduce heat loss *(right)*.

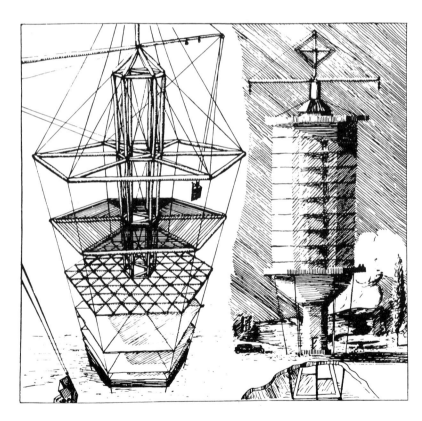

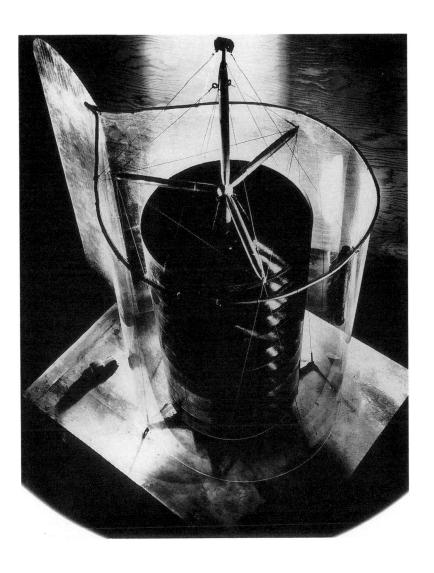

In 1930 a model of the 'Dymaxion' house was shown at the Chicago Arts Club and there was talk of a full-sized example being built for the 1933 World's Fair. By 1930 the specification of the house had changed from the eccentric arrangements described in the patent application. Not only was it now described as 'deliverable in 24 hours' when 'installed and serviced by men trained in their work', but it was said to 'eliminate drudgery, selfishness, exploitation, politics and centralized control', and safeguard against 'flood, fire, tornado, electrical storms, earthquakes and hurricanes'. The construction of the dwelling has become very advanced too. Instead of metal... 'For walls, windows and ceilings: Casein, a transparent, translucent opaque sheeting made from vegetable refuse. The bathrooms are cast in a single sculptural unit of casein and inserted into the house. For doors: Silver balloon silk - inflatable and so dustproof. For shelter covers: Duralumin - an alloy of aluminium used her~ in panels or rollers. For floors: Inflatable rubber units. For light: An oil engine both warms the house and illuminates it by a system of mirrors through the translucent walls.'

The price of this version of the Dymaxion house – when in production – was estimated at $1,500 - approximately £11,000 at 1989 values - at a time when new houses sold for $8,000. In the event, when asked by the organizers of the 1933 World's Fair what it would cost to build a prototype for production, Fuller honestly replied that the figure would be in excess of $100 million, because it had cost Henry Ford $43 million to develop the Model-A, the successor to the famous Model-T car. In the end the World's Fair organizers built a non-mast-supported 'house of tomorrow' with some superficial resemblance to the Dymaxion House instead.

dymaxion cars

'Since I was intent on developing a high-technology dwelling machine that could be air delivered to any remote, beautiful country site where there might be no roadways or landing fields for airplanes, I decided to try to develop an omni-medium transport vehicle to function in the sky, on negotiable terrain, or on water - to be securely landable anywhere, like an eagle'.

Buckminster Fuller 1983

Buckminster Fuller and Starling Burgess built three Dymaxion cars during 1933 and 1934. And unlike the Dymaxion house and the Dymaxion towers, which were destined to remain paper and model projects, there is no doubt about their appearance, existence or date of birth. Although they never intentionally left the ground, the principles underlying their design derived from Fuller's '4-D Auto-Airplane' sketches of 1928, and the subsequent plaster Noguchi models that were lovingly painted by Fuller himself for exhibition in the parking areas beneath the model Dymaxion houses.

The aeroplane ancestry of the Dymaxion cars was plain from the beginning. In his 1928 '4-D Auto-Airplane' sketches Fuller had showed little more than a 'teardrop' aircraft fuselage with an inverted vee-bottom, recessed front wheels and a combined rear steering wheel and aerodynamic rudder. This vehicle was intended to use the roads under the power of two of three 'liquid air turbines', each driving one of the front wheels. A third 'turbine' would drive the nose-mounted propeller for flight. The transport would take to the air by using its forward motion to inflate pneumatic wings, with the pressure topped up by an air pump.

By 1932 the '4-D Auto-Airplane' had developed into the '4-D transport' with twin four cylinder petrol engines, no propeller and no wings. This vehicle still resembled an aeroplane but was intended only to taxi, or 'plane' with its tail lifted off the ground so as to develop 'infinite wheelbase' for comfort and smoothness. We know a lot about the thinking behind this vehicle because it is described - 'weight unloaded approx. 400 lbs, exquisite acceleration and deceleration (as with outboard motorboat racers)' - in some detail in a long and fascinatingly illustrated article entitled 'Streamlining' that Fuller wrote, but did not sign, for the November 1932 issue of *Shelter*. Here the inventor explained that his conception of the car of the future hinged upon weight reduction and streamlining. He was still advocating the unique '4-D' hull form of an inverted vee to achieve aerodynamic stability, but

The genesis of the design of the Dymaxion cars. First crude sketches dating from '4-D' manuscript of 1928 show the 'Auto-Airplane', a high-wing road-going convertiplane with combined steering rudder and tailwheel, plus elevators, propeller and 'inflatable wings' for flight (34). This version has three power units described as 'liquid-air turbines'.

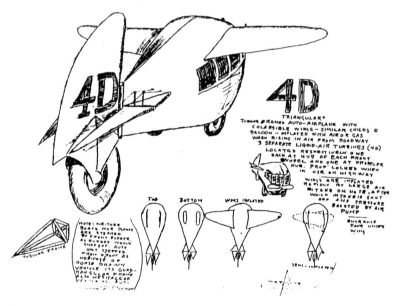

leaned more towards contemporary examples like the Granville brothers' 'Gee Bee' racing monoplanes with their short, stubby fuselages and wire-braced wings. Fuller had clearly learned a lot about aircraft construction techniques. His last '4-D Transport' drawing before the construction of the real thing showed a twin engined tricycle frame with rear wheel steering and a retractable aerofoil steering rudder. The dogged adherence to steering from the rear was explained by the exemplary manoeuvrability of yachts, fish, birds and aeroplanes - as well as being a step towards the eventual possibility of flight.

Clearly money was needed to convert the *Shelter* drawings into a real road-going vehicle, and here Fuller had struck lucky. His Dymaxion house model had aroused the interest of a Philadelphia stock broker named Philip Pearson who had miraculously avoided the consequences of the 1929 Wall Street Crash by liquidating his holdings immediately beforehand. Like many financiers of the time, all of whom had been impressed by Henry Ford's creation of a new industry with his Model-T car only ten years before, Pearson believed that the motor industry was capable of drawing America out of the Depression if only it could make another major design breakthrough.

Impressed by one of Fuller's Dymaxion house models exhibited in an engineering bookshop in New York, Pearson had been advised by an associate William Stout, the designer of the Ford Trimotor airliner and a man who was later to produce his own short-lived dream car, the 'Scarab', that Fuller's ideas about cars too were far ahead of their time. What Stout told Pearson that Fuller could do can be inferred from a report that Fuller published in *Shelter* of an address given by Stout in 1932 to the Society of Automotive Engineers of America entitled 'What Aviation can do for Motor Cars'. According to Stout, the sort of cars America ought to build to recreate prosperity needed to have more interior space within the same track and wheelbase; should be more luxurious, comfortable and silent; should have between 50 and 100 brake horse power; should have 'effortless' steering and automatic

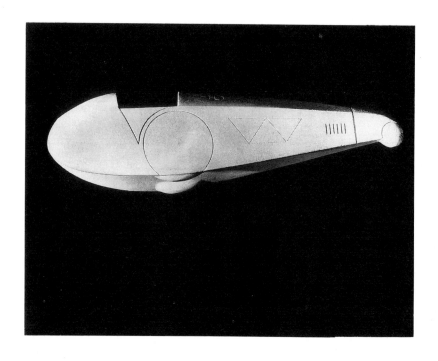

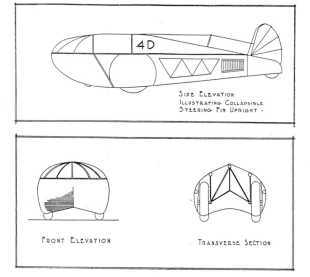

SIDE ELEVATION.
ILLUSTRATING COLLAPSIBLE
STEERING FIN UPRIGHT ·

FRONT ELEVATION

TRANSVERSE SECTION

Later Isamu Noguchi model *(above)* and general arrangement drawings from 1932 *Shelter* magazine *(right)*, show wingless twin-petrol engined '4-D transport' driven through front wheels. Triangulated space-frame chassis and disappearance of rear control surfaces are noteworthy. Important additional design *(left)* from *Shelter* shows retractable aerodynamic 'steering fin' for high speed running.

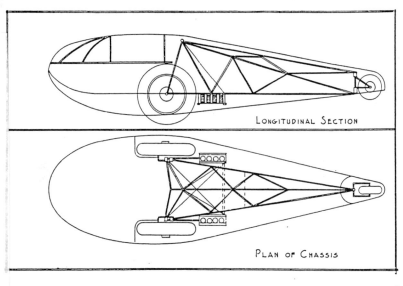

LONGITUDINAL SECTION

PLAN OF CHASSIS

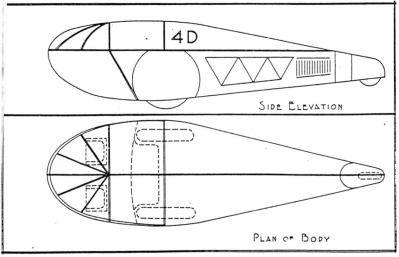

4D

SIDE ELEVATION

PLAN OF BODY

transmission; should accelerate from 0-60 in 3 seconds (*a performance still impossible in any conventional passenger car*); should be air conditioned and achieve a fuel consumption of 30 miles per gallon, and should sell for around $2,000 'on a small production run'.

This, we must presume, is roughly what Pearson had in mind for the Dymaxion car when he financed Fuller with an unspecified quantity of cash in the early spring of 1933, the time of highest incidence of bank and savings failures of the American Depression. Fuller of course still nursed greater long term ambitions for the car including, eventually, vertical take off and high speed flight, but he took the money. Between them, Fuller and Burgess leased a disused auto plant in Bridgeport, Connecticut, and the '4-D Dymaxion' factory opened up for business - not only to build cars but to build Starling Burgess's racing yachts - on March 4th 1933, the day Franklin Delano Roosevelt was inaugurated President of the United States. In a further indication of the state of the United States economy at that time, more than one thousand men applied for the twenty-eight skilled jobs Fuller and Burgess had to offer. Two of the first coachbuilders hired were ex-Rolls Royce employees, survivors of the ill-timed scheme to manufacture Rolls Royce cars in nearby Hartford that had folded with the onset of the Depression. The '4-D Dymaxion' team worked intensively on the prototype and the first revolutionary Dymaxion car was unveiled after only four months, on July 12th 1933. This machine was quickly sold to Gulf Oil with Connecticut licence plate FV 453 and managed, as a promotional vehicle, by a former Navy test pilot named Al Williams. Unfortunately within two months it was involved in a fatal accident that took place at the main gate of the 1933 Chicago World Exposition. It was later repaired with a redesigned, faceted windscreen and again used by Gulf for an unspecified period until it was destroyed in an accidental garage fire at the National Bureau of Standards in Washington DC. This car formed the basis of the Dymaxion car patents in Great Britain and the United States that Fuller applied for in October 1933. They were not granted until 1937.

The '4-D Dymaxion' car factory at Bridgeport, Connecticut, opened by Buckminster Fuller and Starling Burgess on March 4th 1933. A former dynamometer building abandoned by the defunct Locomobile car company it was destined to close down again in little more than a year.

(*Below*) Starling Burgess, key designer of the Dymaxion car project and also engineer of the ten-deck streamlined Dymaxion tower, photographed in the '4-D Dymaxion' factory on 18th July 1933. Burgess's trestle table supports mechanical calculator and hull model of *Enterprise*, his victorious 1930 J-Class Americas Cup defender. Part of the agreement between Fuller and Burgess was that yachts would be built by the same 28-strong labour force.

Under construction at the same time, the 40 foot Burgess sloop *(left)* and the wooden framework for the first Dymaxion car *(below)* show the same unmechanized, craft construction technique. Immense rear suspension A-frame and all-wood tail fairing of car are noteworthy: sides were clad in aluminium and roof 'decked in' with taut 'yacht' canvas tonneau for lightness.

Interior of car *(right)* was finished like a racing yacht, and featured only four seats. Later cars seated up to eleven passengers. Handle above steering wheel controls roof-mounted rear view mirror viewed through perspex panel. The first finished Dymaxion car *(below right)* displayed outside the factory on July 12th 1933, shows superb Burgess streamlining, doors only on left side, perspex windscreen and non opening windows. Button-down canvas tonneau to cabin and rear engine compartment can be clearly seen, as can roof-mounted engine air intake, side-mounted marker light and recess for single headlight.

The second Dymaxion car (original licence plate SI 187) was begun upon completion of the first, and completed shortly after the World's Fair crash. It had a similar canvas roof, but a metal cover over the engine compartment. It differed from FV 453 in having more glass and opening lights, as well as doors in both sides, but the European investors who had wanted to buy it - both of whom were passengers in the first car at the time of the accident - had by then changed their minds. There had also been a difference of opinion with Pearson about a return on his investment and the upshot was that Fuller was obliged to finance the building of the second and third cars himself with money left him by his mother. Car number two was later made over to the Dymaxion labour force in lieu of wages prior to the liquidation sale that ended Dymaxion car production in 1934. This car disappeared for many years and was discovered in an abandoned condition in California in the 1960s. It was later purchased for the Harrah Collection in Reno, Nevada, where it was externally refurbished and still survives.

The third Dymaxion car (original licence plate HF 349) was completed in 1934 just before the company was wound up. Generously provided with engine compartment ventilation in the body sides it was the only Dymaxion with an all-metal roof, flush door handles and no roof-mounted engine cooling air-intake, but was otherwise a virtual copy of car number two. This third car is the one that was photographed carrying passengers at the 1934 Chicago World Exposition where it was a popular item, executing a peculiar rotating 'dance' made possible by its rear-wheel steering. It was later sold to the conductor Leopold Stokowski who only kept it for a few months. After passing through many ownerships the car was rediscovered in Brooklyn in 1944 and repurchased for Fuller by a friend. It was restored at the Beech Aircraft plant in Wichita, Kansas in 1945 where it was photographed alongside Fuller's private plane. It was then sold again and disappeared. The last reliable report of its existence dates from 1950, by which time it had covered more than 300,000 miles.

The aircraft-style streamlining shows clearly in the lines of the first Dymaxion (licence number FV 453) outside the Bridgeport factory in the summer of 1933 with a contemporary Franklin tourer alongside. Starling Burgess and Buckminster Fuller *(below)* standing beside FV 453 at the Roosevelt Airfield, Long Island on July 21st 1933.

25-7-21-33-Starling Burgess & Buckminster Fuller

Famous American racing driver Ralph de Palma standing next to FV 453. This is the only known photograph of the vehicle after the fatal World's Fair accident. In the course of repairs the windscreen was rebuilt according to the less aerodynamic style of the later cars. Problem with wiper coverage can be seen.

Despite their failure to hover or fly, the appearance of the Dymaxion cars was revolutionary, and must remain a subject of fascination for anyone who has ever seen a photograph of one, let alone the sole physical survivor. With the first vehicle in particular, whose single headlamp and non-opening perspex windows made for cleaner lines, Fuller and Burgess had contrived to create one of the most startlingly beautiful and original motor vehicles ever built. A dramatic contrast with all its contemporaries, it was not until the advent of the Porsche 356 fifteen years later that a drastic adherence to the principles of streamlining would again be accompanied by such breathtaking aesthetic success.

FV 453 looked like the wingless, tailless fuselage of the 1928 drawings only better. Although it was hand-built using orthodox coachbuilding techniques it looked like a streamlined monocoque aircraft, its near-perfect teardrop shape broken only by a broad roof-mounted air intake for the engine behind the passenger cabin. Finished in natural aluminium on an ash frame, its 5.7 metre eleven-seat body had a perspex-glazed 'cockpit cover' and doors only on the left hand side. Until the redesign following the crash, sections of the glazing and the canvas roof had to be removed to provide ventilation. At rest, the car stood nose-high, like a tailwheel aircraft of the period. Inside it boasted aircraft seats, with seat belts, and aircraft-style controls and equipment, including an airspeed indicator and a radio. The body was carried on a chrome-molybdenum aircraft steel ladder chassis articulated into two scissors-like sections hinged at the front axle. The forward ladder frame carried the weight of the passengers and the 80 hp V8 rear-mounted engine driving the front pair of wheels. Above and behind it a long, thin A-frame of perforated steel passed either side of the engine carrying the 160 degree-turning rear steering wheel. The engine, gearbox, transmission and running gear were all taken from the contemporary Ford V8, the parts allegedly supplied by Ford at a discount of 70 per cent. One of the most serious limitations of the Ford legacy was the archaic formerly rear, now front, beam axle and transverse leaf spring suspension with its friction dampers. At the rear Fuller duplicated this with a smaller tension-damped transverse leaf springs above which the long A-frame was suspended.

The radically unorthodox layout of the Dymaxion car - Fuller simply turned the Ford differential upside down to make it drive the right way - possessed some advantages over the front engine-rear drive arrangement then almost universal in the motor industry but, as it emerged, many disadvantages too. Its principal gain was low-speed manoeuvrability, with a parking distance only 75 mm longer than the length of the car, and a turning circle only 300 mm greater. Fuller frequently boasted that at 15 mph the car could make a 180 degree turn in a matter of seconds.

The negative side of these achievements emerged at higher speeds. All three Dymaxion cars suffered from control problems above 50 miles per hour. In part this resulted from precisely those design analogies with birds and fish that had spurred their inventor on. Unlike these rear-steering creatures who operate in a single

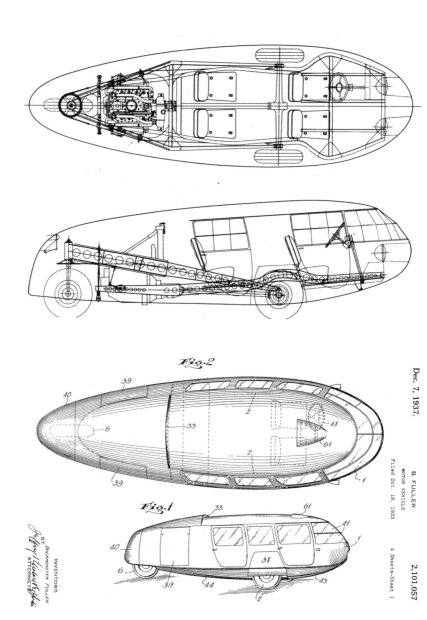

Fig.2

Fig.1

Dec. 7, 1937. B. FULLER 2,101,057

MOTOR VEHICLE

Filed Oct. 18, 1933   4 Sheets-Sheet 1

INVENTORS
BUCKMINSTER FULLER

BY

ATTORNEY

Composite simplified plan and section of the Dymaxion car showing smooth roofline and immense rear A-frame of FV 453 with double headlight arrangement of later cars *(left)*. Patent application drawings *(below)* of October 1933 are also composites, showing increased window area, metal top and roof periscope blister of later cars, coupled with underslung leaf-spring for rear A-frame and single headlight of prototype FV 453.

medium, all cars are interface vehicles, partly moving through the air and partly moving on the ground. The implications of this were clearly appreciated by Fuller - his 1928 drawings of the '4-D Auto-airplane' showed aerodynamic rudder and elevator controls - but he did not foresee its consequences as he might have done. In retrospect this is difficult to understand, because in 1933, as today, all flight training manuals explained to pilots that when taxiing tailwheel aircraft into the wind they should hold the elevators in the 'up' position in order to prevent the tail rising. It is clear from the 1932 *Shelter* drawings that Fuller believed he had dealt with this problem by deleting the tailplane and elevators altogether and providing only a 'retractable air rudder' to take over the steering when the tail rose. But not only was none of the Dymaxion cars ever fitted with such a rudder, the inventor greatly underestimated the tail-lifting effect as well. Even without his unique inverted-vee 'air-keel', as the Dymaxion cars accelerated their tails still tended to rise, just like those of aircraft. The absence of elevator downforce meant there was no

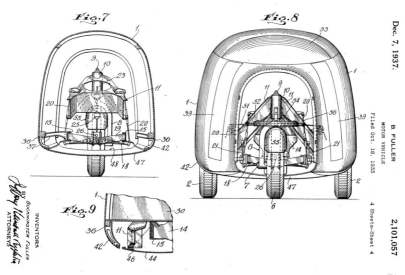

Dec. 7, 1937.

B. FULLER

MOTOR VEHICLE

Filed Oct. 18, 1933

4 Sheets-Sheet 4

2,101,057

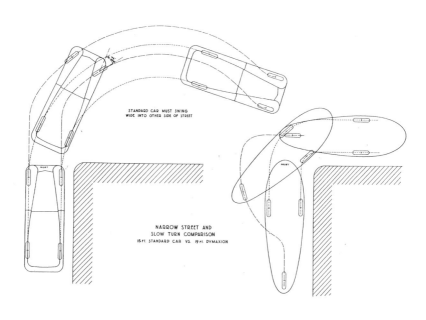

STANDARD CAR MUST SWING
WIDE INTO OTHER SIDE OF STREET

NARROW STREET AND
SLOW TURN COMPARISON
15 FT. STANDARD CAR VS. 19 FT. DYMAXION

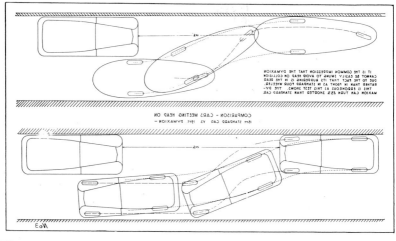

COMPARISON - CARS MEETING HEAD ON
— 15 FT. STANDARD CAR VS. 19 FT. DYMAXION —

IT IS THE COMMON IMPRESSION THAT THE DYMAXION
CANNOT BE EASILY SWUNG TO AVOID HEAD ON COLLISION
DUE TO THE FACT THAT ITS RUDDERING IS IN THE REAR
RATHER THAN IN FRONT AS IN STANDARD FOUR WHEELER.
THIS IS ERRONEOUS AS THIS TEST SHOWS. THE DY-
MAXION CAN TURN 25% SHORTER THAN STANDARD CAR

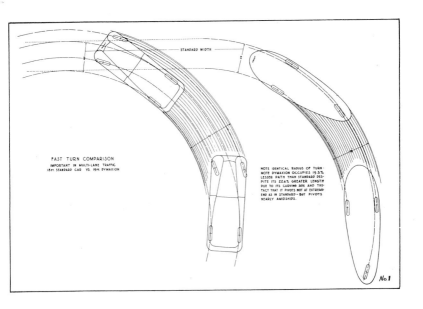

FAST TURN COMPARISON
IMPORTANT IN MULTI-LANE TRAFFIC
15ft. STANDARD CAR VS. 19ft. DYMAXION

NOTE IDENTICAL RADIUS OF TURN.
NOTE DYMAXION OCCUPIES 19.5%
LESSER PATH THAN STANDARD DES-
PITE ITS 22.6% GREATER LENGTH
DUE TO ITS CURVING SIDE AND THE
FACT THAT IT PIVOTS NOT AT EXTREME
END AS IN STANDARD—BUT PIVOTS
NEARLY AMIDSHIPS.

No I

Rationalisations for the superiority of the Dymaxion's tricycle wheel arrangement and rear-wheel steering. Phenomenal turning circle of Dymaxion enables it to make right-angle street turn in less space than a conventional car. Avoiding head-on collisions *(below left)*. The Dymaxion averts disaster by turning in 25 per cent less distance than the conventional car, and consumes less road make a fast, sweeping turn *(above)*. Rear view from Dymaxion's periscope is compared favourably with conventional mirror view through rear window *(right)*.

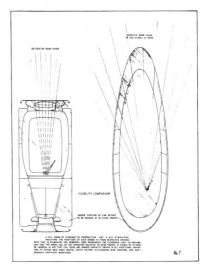

way of controlling this tendency except by reducing speed, for whenever the 'tailwheel' left the ground there was an immediate loss of steering control.

The more this phenomenon is examined, the more surprising Fuller's thinking can be seen to be. Initially, as we know, he had anticipated the tail of the car rising and planned to continue steering by means of an aerodynamic rudder. The implication of this is that he expected the Dymaxion to run at a high speed, perhaps over 100 miles an hour. But here Fuller had far outstripped automobile industry knowledge in 1933. Steering was not the only problem for a road-going vehicle at such speeds. Given a long clear road the loss of ground-contact steering might have been offset by the use of an air rudder, but normal road conditions clearly required the ability to slow down rapidly, as well as run straight and negotiate broad radius turns at high speed. Sooner, rather than later in the trials of the first Dymaxion car, Fuller must have discovered that braking through the narrow footprint of two wheels led to a skid. Even when stationary the weight distribution of the car was 75 per cent front axle: 25 per cent rear wheel. This meant that rear-wheel braking would have been ineffective, and in fact rear-wheel brakes were not fitted to any of the cars. Burgess and Fuller had placed the mass of the engine as far aft and as low down as they could to counteract weight-transfer at speed, but this alone was not sufficient. To make the car work as a high speed '4-D transport', Fuller would have had to fit an entire aircraft tail unit, including elevators, as well as a steering tailwheel and airbrakes.

Even had he taken the opposite tack and devised some means of totally preventing weight-transfer away from the tailwheel, Fuller's stability problems would not have been over. FV 453 demonstrated another and more subtle danger when cornering. The concentration of weight at the rear of the car, coupled with an inevitable flexing of the long and ungainly lever arms that carried the rear suspension from their pivot point at the front axle, created a twisting effect that applied unwanted camber changes to the tailwheel - thus changing its effective steering angle. This, plus the vehicle's aerodynamic tendency always to turn into the wind, not only made steering hazardous but contributed to phenomenal tyre wear. IS 187 and HF 349 were both fitted with a revised and lighter A-frame to counteract this effect but to no avail. On HF 349 the angle of incidence of the 'rudder post' of the rear wheel was changed five times in an unsuccessful attempt to design-out the involuntary cornering camber changes. Other minor faults relating to the basic design included poor backward visibility. All the Dymaxion cars had perspex widows in their roofs through which the driver was supposed to see behind him by way of an external driving mirror called by Fuller a 'periscope'. The extensive fitment of what would nowadays be called 'Nerf Bars' to HF 349 suggests that this arrangement was inadequate for manoeuvring in confined spaces. Furthermore FV 453 in its pre-accident form had no windscreen wipers, while HF 349 and SI 187 were fitted with up to four wipers in an attempt to sweep different parts of their large faceted windscreens.

Burgess and Fuller made great efforts to deal with these chronic design faults, but never to the extent of abandoning the chassis/body in favour of a genuine aircraft monocoque, or changing the rear-wheel steering arrangement. In retrospect it is clear that the development of the basic vehicle into a kind of high-speed motorway cruiser, steered aerodynamically like a taxiing aeroplane and braked by some as yet undevised anti-dive system, was beyond their powers. Instead minor palliatives were initiated. The designers decided to replace the long steering cables, which ran through turning blocks as on a yacht, with heavier ones to prevent them stretching, but this was never done. They also intended to raise the steering ratio, a laborious 20:1, to a remarkable 30:1 if further examples were built - yet another example of the incompatibility of high and low speed steering characteristics that was endemic in the design without its air·rudder. On SI 187 and HF 349 a lock was inserted that had to be lifted manually before turns requiring the rear of the vehicle to move outside the track of the front wheels could be executed.

The only surviving Dymaxion car is vehicle number two (originally licence number SL 187), seen here in the condition in which it was discovered *(left)* and after removal to the Harrah Collection in Reno, Nevada. Externally restored, the car is frequently exhibited, here *(below)* at the opening of the Museum of Science and Industry in Chicago in 1973.

This replaced FV 453's 'audible warning device' that had proved insufficient.

Over the years a legend has grown up about the performance of the Dymaxion cars. Fuller himself claimed to have broken the lap record 'by more than 50 per cent' at an unspecified 'midget car stadium in the Bronx' in a Dymaxion. In an appearance at the Roosevelt Raceway, Long Island on the 11th of August 1933, FV 453 was announced as being capable of 120 mile an hour, but no timings were released. As late as July 1988 Automobile Magazine in the United States claimed that the car could reach 120 miles an hour with fuel consumption in the 25-30 miles per gallon range.

In fact, despite Fuller's understanding of the importance of power to weight ratios, the kerb weight of the Dymaxions was never revealed or, possibly, never even calculated. It must however have been well in excess of 2,000 kilograms and, at such a weight, with a slow-revving side-valve 85 bhp V8 driving through a three-speed gearbox and standard 3.57:1 Ford rear axle, it can safely be said that the claimed figures are impossible.

By the autumn of 1934, with Pearson's money and Fuller's inheritance consumed, there were no more customers for Dymaxion cars. The '4-D Dymaxion' factory was closed down and all its assets were sold in a sheriff's liquidation sale - a common fate for industrial enterprises during the Great Depression. Fuller parted company with Burgess and removed his family to New York where he started work on his first real book, a volume that was to be printed three years later under the enigmatic title *Nine Chains to the Moon*.

There were however two sequels to the Dymaxion car episode. Throughout the 1930s Fuller remained in an uncertain relationship with the major American automobile companies, notably with Chrysler, Packard and Studebaker, then independent manufacturers, all of whom had expressed guarded interest in developing the Dymaxion car further. There was still the conviction, mentioned earlier, that the motor industry could be used to lever the American economy out of the Depression provided a new breakthrough in car design could be made. Susceptible to this thinking was an investment group named Hayden Stone that had inherited the barely solvent Curtiss Wright aeronautical corporation and the defunct Pierce Arrow car company. Hayden Stone proposed to finance the production of a new 'Curtiss Wright Dymaxion' at the Pierce Arrow Plant in Buffalo, using the proceeds from the sale of airfields belonging to Curtiss Wright to finance the operation. Although these negotiations foundered at a late stage, some detailed models of proposed Dymaxion derivatives, ranging from tiny 300 mm styling exercises to a 4.2 metre full-size buck, were built by Joseph Kuthmeyer in New York for exhibition at the 1939 World's Fair. These models were destroyed during World War Two. All that survives of this stillborn project are Fuller's general arrangement drawings for a four-seat 'Tudor Sportster' and a single seater traffic car.

The last revival of the Dymaxion car was a project called the D-45, which surfaced in 1943. It began when the industrialist Henry J. Kaiser invited Fuller to make proposals for a revolutionary new car for post-war production. As a result of his work as Director of Mechanical Engineering for the United States Board of Economic Warfare at the time, Fuller had little leisure for the task, but he was loath to let the possibility pass by so he persuaded an engineer named Walter Sanders and an unnamed architect to help him.

The vehicle that emerged from their wartime design effort was even more radical than its predecessors. Short and wide, its length 3 metres and its width over 2 metres, the proposed D-45 was still of a pleasant aerodynamic form even though its great width permitted four-abreast seating. The vehicle still adhered stubbornly to the three-wheel Dymaxion layout, but Fuller proposed to correct all the problems of rear-wheel steering by the dramatic method of providing two separate steering systems. A normal steering wheel would control the front wheels at speed on the open road, while a separate crank handle could turn the rear wheel for close-quarters manoeuvrability. The handling problems posed by the excessive weight and primitive beam axle and leaf spring suspension of the earlier vehi-

ALL OUT AID
TO GREAT BRITAIN
AND THE ALLIES

Dymaxion car number three (licence plate HF 349) soon after completion *(left)*, and performing at the 1934 Chicago World's Fair *(right)*, where Buckminster Fuller (in white suit) is shown helping passengers through the rear door. The car differed from its predecessor in having an all-metal roof with a fin-shaped engine exhaust tunnel, more opening glass area, vertical door shut-lines and recessed door catches. Car number three was sold to the conductor Leopold Stokowski and was still in use in New York in 1942 for advertising purposes. Discovered abandoned in Brooklyn in 1945 it was shipped to Wichita, Kansas and restored for Fuller's own use. Here *(below)* it is shown alongside Fuller's own Republic Seabee amphibian. After the collapse of Fuller Houses Inc. the car was sold and disappeared.

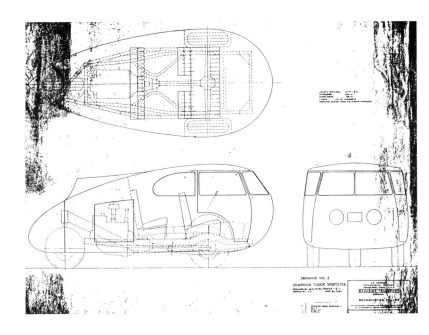

DRAWING NO. 2

DYMAXION TUDOR SPORTSTER

DYMAXION TRANSPORT

BUCKMINSTER FULLER

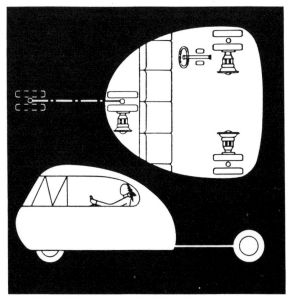

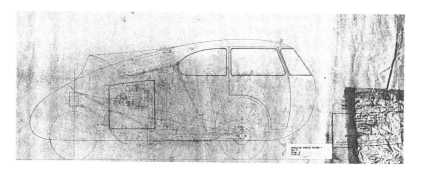

Putative successors to the Dymaxion that never went into production were the 4.2 metre V-8 powered 'Tudor Sportster' *(left)* and the even smaller single seater *(below)*. The Kaiser-sponsored D-45 represented the most advanced version of the car *(above)* version of the car was to have been powered by three gas turbines driving through hydraulic pumps, with three-wheel steering and an extendable tail-boom for high-speed comfort.

cles were to be solved by the adoption of all-metal monocoque construction and a hydro-pneumatic independent suspension system similar in performance to that introduced on the revolutionary French Citroen DS19 in 1955. The inherent three-wheel car problems of 'pitching' and tyre-wear were to be solved by an even more radical departure. Instead of a long wheel base as on the earlier Dymaxion cars, the D-45 achieved great economies in weight and streamlining by mounting its rear steering wheel on the end of an extendible boom. In the D-45 the mythical 'infinite wheelbase' of the original '4-D Auto-Airplane', which was to have been steered by an air rudder, would be achieved without loss of ground contact by extending the tail boom rearward as speed increased. At low speeds with the boom retracted, as Fuller already knew, the car would be safe and phenomenally manoeuvrable using rear-wheel steering.

The twin steering systems and extending wheelbase were not the sole innovations of the proposed Kaiser D-45. Partially reverting to his multi-engine 1932 design, Fuller proposed to replace the old Dymaxion rear-mounted single water cooled engine with no less than three tiny air-cooled radial five-cylinder 25 brake horse power petrol engines, one to drive each of the wheels. According to the only drawings and descriptions that remain in the Fuller archive, these small engines were intended to run at a constant speed and each drive a hydraulic pump powering the adjacent wheel. Conventional throttle control would be replaced by a method of varying the volume of hydraulic fluid supplied to each pump. In order to limit the noise level of three engines running at optimum power, Fuller intended to use varying numbers of them at any one time. For acceleration or hill climbing all engines would be used: for high speed cruising the power supply could be cut back until only the boomed out tail motor was driving. In this way Fuller also hoped to achieve a very low overall fuel consumption.

In a final version of the D-45 project published after the war, Fuller proposed the installation of three gas turbines driving all-steering twin road wheels in place of the three petrol engines and the two separate steering systems. Fuller's own description of this last of all Dymaxion car designs is characteristic:-

'With the one-half-pound-per-horse-power gas turbine coming of age, the trend is to re-explore promptly the possibilities of earth-bound vehicles. The latest Dymaxion features coupled-steering of all three 'duo-tired' wheel assemblies. Each wheel assembly contains its own gas turbine. The fuselage is suspended by three aircraft type vertical aerol struts, and has a retractable rear wheel tail boom for lengthening the wheelbase at speed. It is seven feet wide and ten feet long (contracted) with cross-wind 'fairing.' It has a seven foot driving divan, convertible into a large bed. It may 'revolve into' half the parking length of present cars. The top is a convertible aluminium water melon type. It has a faired belly with high ground clearance for field work, will 'gun' high speed turns without skid. Weight 960 lbs (440 kg).'

Years later it became clear that Kaiser had in fact proceeded with the 1943 project in his own way. After a preliminary agreement with the inventor was not taken up, he placed the development of the D-45 in the hands of a former Chevrolet engineer named Alexander Taub. A much modified vehicle which had reverted to a single engine and abandoned the extendable rear boom, was tested and abandoned in 1946. But by this time Buckminster Fuller was hard at work in Wichita, Kansas, on the most advanced house of the 20th century.

house of the century

'Richard Buckminster Fuller is a chunky, powerful little man with a build like a milk bottle, a mind that functions like a cross between a roll-top desk and a jet-propulsion motor, and one simple aim in life: to remake the world. Into a mere fifty years he has crammed enough technical careers to staff the faculty of a sizeable engineering school, and by way of extra curricular activity has managed to write several books, publish a magazine, and create a system of mathematics. As a cartographer he is unique: he is the first man to be granted a US patent for a basically new method of map projection. These achievements, however may all fade into obscurity if his current venture · a house · succeeds, for this 'dwelling machine' is likely to produce greater social consequences than the introduction of the automobile.'

Fortune magazine, April 1946

The great architectural obsession of the first half of the 20th century was the factory-built home, or 'repro-shelter' as it was called by the SSA, the initials of 'Structural Study Associates', a group of American Modern architects who by 1932 had found their natural focus in *Shelter* magazine. This expensive 2,500 circulation radical architectural monthly, carrying no advertising and by modern standards very few illustrations, was published in Philadelphia by Richard Buckminster Fuller.

In the great catastrophe of the Depression in America, with its unprecedented slump in agricultural prices, massive mortgage foreclosures, collapsed investment, industrial bankruptcy, unemployment, poverty, and the creation of a vast homeless and migrant underclass, the SSA was an unheeded splinter group in a sea of radical urban politics, and *Shelter* itself but a short-lived 'little magazine'. In the cruel economic reality of workless 1932 both were little more than an avant-garde design offshoots of a tiny movement called 'Technocracy' founded ten years before by a New York engineer named Howard Scott. 'Technocracy' was one of the profusion of alternative social ideas that flourished in the desperation of Depression America, one of a number of movements that attracted and repelled followers throughout the 1930s. Fuller and the SSA found their place at the outer rim of this intellectual and political firmament, further out even than Scott and 'Technocracy'. But while Scott was destined

Ten years that transformed the life of Buckminster Fuller. The 'Three Hours for Lunch Club' in session in New York, 1935 *(right)*. Depression thinking in progress between (left to right), Meredith Blagden, Richard Buckminster Fuller, Haley Fiske and Chris Seller. A decade later Fuller is part of the aviation 'reconversion' industry in Wichita, Kansas. Here *(below)*, he swings the prop of a Luscombe Silvaire light plane.

to end up as no more than an historical footnote to now forgotten demagogues like Upton Sinclair, Huey Long, Doctor Townsend and Father Coughlin, Fuller's real fame was still to come.

Started on an extremely modest scale in 1918, Scott's movement had at first called itself 'Technical Alliance'. At that time it was a loosely connected research group of scientists and engineers 'studying the physical operations of society on the continent of North America', as Scott put it in his book *An Introduction to Technocracy*. In 1932, the year of Fuller's most complete involvement in *Shelter*, this research group reformed under the title of 'Technocracy Incorporated', as a non-profit, non-political organization funded in part by the Architects Emergency Relief Fund with offices at Columbia University. The ARF too was a Depression organization, formed to help the large number of architects who had been thrown out of work. Some of its demands, including taking over unlet commercial skyscrapers for housing, or recreating 1932 Los Angeles Olympic Villages as low-cost housing projects all over the United States, were enthusiastically supported by the SSA and Fuller himself in the pages of his magazine.

In 1932 'Technocracy, Inc.' was on the brink of its greatest success. In the following year, while Fuller was in Connecticut building the Dymaxion cars, Scott's organization was preaching what amounted to a new religion to an increasing number of believers. In the pages of his book 'An Introduction to Technocracy' - a far less congested and more controlled argument than Fuller had mustered up to that time - Scott was expounding his seductive Spenglerian belief that the United States in the depths of the Depression was like a stalled engine. The economy, he said, was no more than a machine and if it was rebuilt according to sound engineering principles it would soon start running again.

What 'Technocracy' proposed was that the free market should be abolished in favour of a scientifically constant measure of money in the form of energy. All goods and services were to be given a value in energy units called 'ergs', the value to be determined by the amount of energy used in their production. This economic system called for payments to be made in 'energy certificates' which would expire at the end of every year, whether they had been used to 'buy' other goods and services or not. The minimum 'energy certificate' would be the number of 'ergs' earned by 16 hours of labour a week. The 'erg' currency would be held, issued and administered by the banks, just like paper money.

Apart from the new energy currency, the most significant aspect of the 'Technocracy' plan was the creation of a new ruling class consisting of engineers, scientists and technologists. Every detail of day to day living for the masses was to be worked out by these experts so as to maximize efficiency and eliminate waste, and it was here that prefabrication was to play a vital part. In the interests of energy efficiency the Technocrats proposed the abolition of the conventional permanent single family house in favour of lightweight, mast-supported prefabricated apartment dwellings with communal facilities. An article in the movement's own magazine '*The Technocrat*' entitled 'A tantalizing glimpse of your home in a Technate' - the 'Technocracy' version of a city - explained that such housing would not be designed by stylistically-oriented architects 'from the Moorish, English, Chateau, or any other 1,000 year-old style they try to follow', but by 'experts who have devoted a lifetime to researching the most comfortable, convenient and livable machine in which to live... So-called Modernistic architecture designed entirely for 'looks' would be also be discarded in favour of 'the simplest geometrical forms that will fit your functional requirements'. The article concluded that 'Experiments have shown that such a streamlined functional dwelling is actually much more pleasing to the modern eye than any of the old world baroque ornamental and ceremonial designs that have been handed down to us from the age of scarcity'.

'Technocracy, Inc.' peaked in 1933, never having attracted a membership of more than 20,000, and in later years Fuller was at pains to show that he had never been a member, or in any way associated with Scott himself. Nonetheless it is interesting to consider the similarities between the two men's thinking. Not only does the 'Technate' described in *The Technocrat* closely resembles the 'city of 4-D towers' illustrated in Buckminster Fuller's 1928 manifesto, but the criticism of conventional and 'so-called Modernistic' architecture echoes his own intemperate terminology almost to the letter. Conversely, the energy economy outlined by Scott embodies key elements of the raw-material recycling programme called for by Fuller in his 1938 book *Nine Chains to the Moon*, and leads logically to the principle of design ephemeralization that Fuller was later to elevate to the status of a law of technology. Furthermore Scott's starting point of 'studying the physical operations of society on the continent of North America', is exactly what Fuller did later during his 1938-40 technical consultancy for *Fortune* magazine, aggregating a vast amount of data on energy, population and resources. It was this labour that led to the 'World Energy Map' of 1940, the *Life* magazine world strategy map of 1943 and, eventually, to the patented 'Dymaxion Air Ocean Map' of 1954.

At the height of Scott's movement Fuller was already a contributor to *Fortune* and an earnest proselytizer for the cause of prefabricated housing - 'the industry that industry forgot' - as a pump-priming catalyst for the ailing economy. If he felt that many of his ideas had been appropriated by 'Technocracy, Inc.' he never said so. It was one of his post-'year of silence' principles not to engage in European-style ideological battles head-on. 'I don't fight forces, I use them', as he put it. In any case the kind of resource-control and allocation that was preached by 'Technocracy' hinged upon an assumed but unproven technical capability. It was as much with the triumphant demonstration of the feasibility of mass housing by prefabrication, as with the

One of the twelve prototype copper 'Dymaxion bathrooms' of 1936 that Fuller designed and patented for the Phelps-Dodge Corporation. Executed in fibre glass in Germany after the war the design was finally successful twenty years later.

creation of an inventory of world resources, that Fuller chiefly concerned himself after the liquidation of the '4-D Dymaxion' factory at Bridgeport and his return to New York. In fact the physical manifestations of Dymaxion design that came next owed nothing directly to the agitation of 'Technocracy', the SSA or the ARF. They came about as a consequence of Fuller's *Fortune* connection and a consultancy with the Phelps-Dodge Copper Company, then the third largest copper company in the world. In 1936, in the interests of exploring the development of prefabricated components for housing, Phelps-Dodge commissioned Fuller to design and assemble twelve prototype bathroom units based loosely on the assemblies he had proposed for the later versions of the Dymaxion house. The Phelps Dodge prototypes were pre-plumbed, pre-hand-welded sheet copper installations that could never have been economically produced, but they attracted the hostile attention of organized labour when one or two were used in 'so-called Modernistic' houses as demonstration projects, including a house designed by Richard Neutra on Long Island. Fuller's own work on the design of the bathroom ceased in 1938 and the Phelps-Dodge copper bathroom never went into production, but a very similar design in fibre glass was produced in Germany in the 1950s. Fuller himself returned to the same project in 1940 when he added a capsule containing a fully-fitted kitchen and a small diesel generator and turned the whole package into something that he called a 'Mechanical Wing' for a special issue of *Architectural Forum* called 'The Design Decade'. The 'Mechanical Wing' was a trailer device for towing behind a car with electric power, a reserve water tank, integral cooking and sanitary facilities that was ready to 'plug in' next to a tent or cabin.

In the same year as the proposal for the 'Mechanical Wing' something better than a tent or cabin came along. As part of the second 'New Deal' public spending programme the United States government had introduced an agricultural price-support system that required the production and distribution of thousands of cheap corrugated steel grain storage bins. The Butler

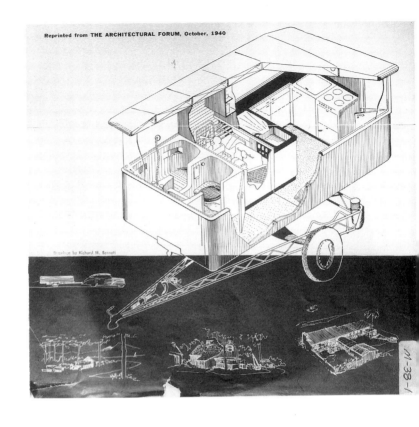

Drawings by Richard M. Bennett

Manufacturing Company of Kansas won the contract and soon its standard 5.5 metre diameter Butler bins were a common sight throughout the Midwest. Fuller saw some of the bins from a car one day and realized that by providing doors and windows, and by fitting 'Dymaxion bathroom units' or connecting them to 'mechanical wings', the cheap enclosures could be converted into small houses. In this way dwellings could be produced in hundreds of thousands at a fraction of the cost and time required for conventional construction. He went on to explore the possibility of joining more than one bin together to make a larger house.

In 1940 Fuller converted the bathroom into the core of a kitchen and electrical generator-equipped 'Mecahnical Wing' project for the magazine *Architectural Forum*.

This was the origin of the 'Dymaxion Deployment Unit' or 'DDU'.

While the first production orders were from Europe during the period of American neutrality before Pearl Harbor, the DDU was planned to be produced in a number of forms, some military and some civilian. In the event the entire production run was bought by the United States Signal Corps as emergency accommodation for radar crews in 1942. Prior to the embargo on the use of steel for non-strategic purposes that followed, the DDU was manufactured by Butler at the rate of 1,000 units a day. Most of the Signal Corps units eventually ended up as transit aircrew accommodation in the Middle East.

The design of the DDU was neither as simple, nor as unsophisticated as it seemed. The subtlety consisting in two unique features, both of which were to play an even larger role in the later 'Wichita' house. The first was an unusual assembly system, quite different to that originally employed by Butler, which called for a removable central mast. This permitted a new compound curved conical roof made of radiating steel segments to be assembled and raised before the walls were hung from it. The second feature was a remarkable ventilation system using a central roof extractor and vertical convention currents from the floor that allegedly enabled the interior of what was little more than a tin drum to remain cool in tropical climates.

Fuller's life as an itinerant design and production consultant and technical advisor to Time Inc., publishers of *Fortune* and *Life* magazines, had ended with his two years of work on the DDU, most of which had been carried out at the Butler production plant in Kansas City. But with the coming of wartime Federal controls over all strategic materials in 1942 he left Butler and turned his attention again to the development of a global cartographic projection suitable for the presentation of the global struggle. In that year he developed the successful version of the 'Dymaxion World Map' that was published in *Life* magazine in March 1943.

Throughout this period Fuller strove to employ his talents more directly in the war effort but without

success. In addition to occasional work for *Life* and *Fortune* he was obliged to survive on consultancy work for Henry J. Kaiser on post-war projects until the very end of 1943, when he at last received a Washington appointment as chief of the mechanical engineering section of the Industrial Engineering Division of the United States Board of Economic Warfare. It was this 'hostilities only' position that was to lead to the triumph and tragedy of the Wichita house - the nearest Fuller ever came to achieving the Structural Studies Associates' dream of mass produced 'repro-shelter'.

Between the lowly DDU and the technological tour de force of the Wichita house there appears to be a much larger gap than there is in reality, for although the Wichita house used a much larger number of components and was built of aircraft duralumin instead of steel, it embodied exactly the same structural principles. As the assembly photographs of the prototype show, the larger and more complex double-curvature roof of the Wichita was made and assembled in exactly the same way as that of the DDU, with the same temporary erection mast and an even larger and more elaborate extract ventilator spinning on Cadillac wheel bearings over the central aperture. In this, as in other ways, the Wichita house of 1946 was the consummation of all that Buckminster Fuller had learned about dwelling design and industrial production since he had drawn those quaint 'mediaeval' drawings of the mast-hung 'Dymaxion house' nearly 18 years before.

The 'Wichita' house came about as an indirect result of Fuller's wartime job. Mindful of the certainty of massive redundancies in the war industries once the conflict ended, and sure of the return of the pre-war housing shortage, in 1944 he submitted a memorandum to the Board of Economic Warfare on what would nowadays be called a 'reconversion programme' for the adaptation of redundant military aircraft factories into facilities for the production of civilian goods, in this case lightweight, prefabricated housing. In the process of drafting his recommendations, Fuller had discussed the matter with several leading American trades unionists. The upshot was that Harvey Brown, presi-

Based on standard cone-top 5.5 metre Butler steel grain bin manufactured for the New Deal farm support programme, the Dymaxion Deployment Unit, or DDU, involved the design of a new curved segmental monocoque roof to provide headroom, and the introduction of windows and a convection ventilation system. Promoted originally as a military accomodation module *(above)* for export to Europe in 1940, before the United States entered the war, the DDU was soon developed into a mass production transportable low cost housing system. Erected roof first on a temporary mast at its destination, the fully furnished steel unit was used strapped down to a timber pallet base.

(Overleaf). Internally *(below)* the DDU was lined up to roof height and internally divided with canvas curtains. Used in some numbers for aircrew transit in the Middle East *(right)* the all-steel DDUs make a contrast with more conventional United States plywood temporary accomodation, like these Palace Corporation houses *(right, below)* for aircraft workers.

97

dent of the International Association of Machinists, the largest aviation labour union, recommended that he approach the Beech Aircraft Corporation of Wichita, Kansas, the manufacturer with the best labour relations in the industry, to explore the possibility of putting such a programme into effect there.

Fuller visited Wichita in 1944 and made a thorough presentation of his ideas to Jack Gaty, senior vice-president and general manager of Beech Aircraft. Gaty became convinced of the viability of lightweight prefabricated housing and insisted on Fuller making a presentation to the workforce as well. This presentation was recorded and has since been published in transcript. It was so successful that at the end of four hours workers and management unanimously endorsed the housing plan.

In the event Fuller's work in Wichita, where he was coincidentally briefly reunited with the former Stokowski Dymaxion car before it finally disappeared, was to absorb the next two years of his life and culminate in a spectacular design achievement. Unhappily it also led to a business catastrophe rivalling that of the 'Stockade Building Company' twenty years before.

When Buckminster Fuller moved to Wichita in October 1944 he left his wife and daughter behind him but took along his young personal assistant Cynthia Lacey. He was 50 years old and had been immersed in the material culture of machine production for nearly a quarter of a century. In that time his experience of failure had been comprehensive. He had been betrayed by stockholders; cold-shouldered by learned professions; frustrated by organized labour and put out of business by government rationing. Despite all these setbacks he was at the height of his powers, confident - arrogant even - in his understanding of the strategic significance of what he was trying to do, and better equipped than any living designer to undertake it. By 1944 his grasp of the 'more for less-ing' structural possibilities of lightweight envelopes using tensile metal in was unequalled. This time he would bypass the reactionary professionals of the construction industry; vault beyond the impoverished model-making of

Members of the famous Wichita house team. Fuller at the time of his move from Washington to Kansas in 1944, 'powerful, confident, like another Henry Ford' *(right)*. Herman Wolf, ex-Washington PR man and briefly president of 'Fuller Houses Inc', and the enigmatic Cynthia Lacey. Wolf was later to make a last-ditch attempt to prevent the collapse of the company by telling Anne Hewlett Fuller that Fuller was having an affair with Lacey. Characteristically the photograph of Wolf and Lacey illustrates a device invented by Fuller to enable several persons to use the single telephone allowed under wartime regulations.

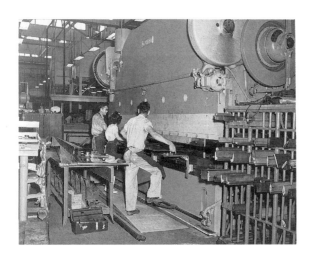

The dramatic scope of the 'Wichita' plan. House components sufficient for a production rate of 60,000 units a year were to be made in this Beech Aircraft factory *(left)* where house parts can be seen in the foreground. The machine tools designed for making airframe parts, like this metal brake shown forming floor beams, could all be adapted.
'Industrial Strategy Map' *(below)* shows scale of air-freighting export plans - 'Australia 7,800 miles', 'Africa 4,700 miles', 'Havana 1,100 miles' etc. - in addition to all United States destinations.

the 'Dymaxion house' years; overleap even the state of the art technology of the automobile and the racing yacht - and match pound for pound and cubic foot for cubic foot the tremendous strength and lightness and productivity of the aviation industry.

Unwilling to risk the labour unrest that had haunted him at Bridgeport, Fuller began by enlisting the aid of the labour unions represented in the housebuilding industry. He invited three of their leaders to join the board of his company 'Fuller Houses Inc.', which was set up with the issue of 15,500 shares of stock at $10 per share. The president was one of Fuller's Washington associates, a former War Production Board public relations officer named Herman Wolf. The vice-president and company secretary was Cynthia Lacey. Fuller reserved for himself the role of chief designer and engineer with a personal holding of 5,500 shares and a veto over all decisions relating to production matters.

As with the Dymaxion car project of ten years before, the initial design work proceeded at a rapid rate. And

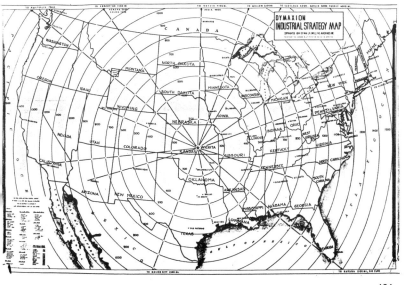

The design evolution of the 1945 Wichita House can be traced back sixteen years to Fuller's mast-supported 'Dymaxion' house models (see p. 50). Concentric-ring wire wheel model *(left)*(81) shows tension wire and compression ring structural principle using same stress pattern as the sheet metal-structured DDU. Alternative system using semi-geodesic framing and triangulated mast *(below)* was soon abandoned.

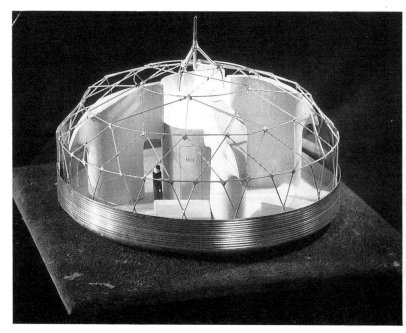

Final model *(right)*, which still survives, shows compound curved duralumin segment roof surmounted by rotating extract ventilator. Despite low stance, house was actually guyed down onto sprung central mast with perimeter rainwater gutter attached to base of wall. Interior of model *(below)* shows spacious plan with two bedrooms, twin dymaxion bathrooms and unique mechanical closets. One of the two living room balconies masks the kitchen.

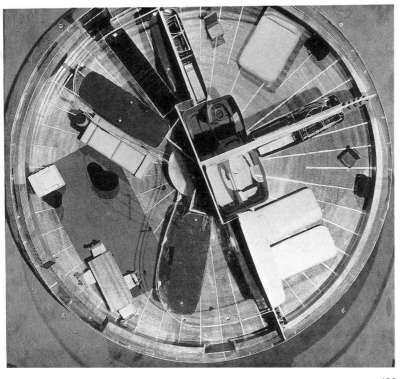

when the time arrived to produce the components for the first full-size houses, access to strategic materials like duralumin and perspex during wartime was facilitated by an order from the US Army Air Corps for two prototypes. 'Soft' tooling for the 'Wichita' houses was hand made by Beech Aircraft craftsmen in an annexe to the main factory. At first Fuller employed only a small number of the 20,000 Beech employees, but as word leaked out most of the remainder looked forward to working on the production of houses as soon as the War ended. In fact it was only two months after the dropping of the Hiroshima bomb and the surrender of Japan when the first prototype was ready, by which time news of the Beechcraft 'reconversion' programme had spread throughout the aircraft industry and hundreds of thousands of workers were eagerly anticipating its success and emulation elsewhere.

When it was finally unveiled, the first 'Wichita' prototype was universally praised as a masterpiece of design, even by the twenty-eight wives of Beech Aircraft workers who were taken on a tour of it and interrogated by journalists afterwards. Twenty-six of them praised its 'beauty' and all of them agreed that it could be spring-cleaned in half an hour. The house really did look as though it was a product of the same industry that had manufactured the P-38 and B-29 and had none of the compromised appearance of the British AIROH house, an uneasy exercise in conventional housing in bolt-together aluminium sections that was going into production on a former bomber production line in England at the same time.

In all the public reactions evoked by the 'Wichita' house there was no sign of the supposed conservatism and preference for traditional styling that had influenced the American housebuilding industry's prewar attempts at prefabrication. Like the Airstream Trailer, a more fortunate design of the period, the 'Wichita' house proved that the public enthusiasm for innovation and performance that had for so long underpinned the research and development of the motor industry, could be ignited in the housing market too. Wolf was a master of publicity, not just locally or

The construction of the prototype Wichita House in 1945 commences with the floor, assembled from radiating duralumin segments enclosed by a riveted ring beam and shown here temporarily supported. Next came the insertion of the erection mast *(below)* and the rigging of the concentric compression rings.

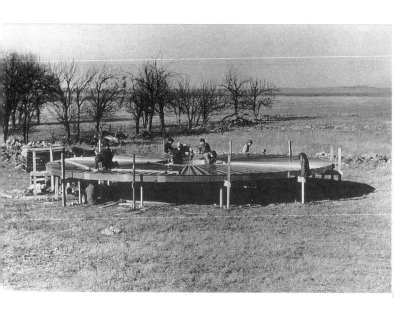

With the roof assembly still at floor level *(left)*, foil moisture barrier, cladding ribs and roofing gores are fitted into place. Completed roof is then hauled up erection mast with truck-mounted safety boom to counteract wind force *(below)*. Diagonal tensile wires rigidize roof-floor assembly when roof is raised and secured. Window mullions and insulated duralumin cladding panels are then riveted into place around the perimeter while specially formed ladder gives access to roof *(right)*.

nationally but worldwide. Between the first press reports and photographs of the house that were released in October 1945 and the end of the campaign in April 1946 no less than 37,000 unsolicited orders for 'Wichita' houses were received by 'Fuller Houses Inc.'

The house that had brought about this avalanche of enthusiasm was a spectacular achievement in industrial design and technology transfer. Using aircraft materials and techniques its performance per pound weight surpassed any conventional construction industry dwelling and, at the production rate of 60,000 units a year that the Beech Aircraft Corporation announced it could achieve, it promised to present a massive challenge to the United States housebuilding industry: a challenge in fact that the housebuilding industry would have been no more able to meet than the horse-drawn transport industry had been to meet the challenge of Henry Ford. As far as can be judged from the reactions and criticisms of the period, the design of the 'Wichita' house had none of the basic flaws that had dogged that of the 'Dymaxion' cars. Instead it went further and solved problems that the conventional construction industry still regarded as 'Acts of God'. The gleaming double-curvature circular roof of the house, assembled top-down on a tensile frame like a bicycle wheel suspended from an assembly mast, was capped with an aerodynamic rotating ventilator designed to 'valve off pressure' like a steam valve in low pressure mid-Western tornado conditions (when conventional houses to this day often 'explode' from excess internal air pressure). The 'Wichita' house was twice the diameter of the 'DDU', and far more elegant and streamlined in its appearance and detailing. Its milium-insulated duralumin and perspex envelope enclosed over 1,000 square feet of centrally heated and air conditioned floor space. Its floor deck was corrugated metal topped with an insulating layer and a wooden internal finish, reminiscent in a way of the unorthodox flooring system proposed for the original '4-D' patent house of eighteen years before. For its occupants it provided automatic natural ventilation with air filtering, electrically operated roller cupboards, movable partitions, plumbed-in vacuum cleaning, a fully-fitted kitchen, two bedrooms and two 'Dymaxion' bathrooms linked to the load-bearing service core at the centre of the house.

Carpeted and tiled, internally painted and furnished, the 'Wichita' house still weighed less than 3,500 kilograms and was costed for production purposes by Beech Aircraft estimators at only $1,800 per unit. In its transportable knock-down component form the whole house fitted into a reusable stainless steel shipping tube that could be carried by a truck or a DC-4 cargo plane anywhere in the world. No component weighed more than 5 kilograms so, on arrival it could be assembled in one day by a team of six, or even by one man with a truck working alone. Most astonishingly its retail price including site and assembly labour, anywhere in the United States, was estimated to be $6,500 at a time when conventional houses of a similar floor area cost at least $12,000. In 1989 terms the equivalent figure might be $50,000 or £33,000: less than half the going rate for the most technologically advanced house imaginable.

At that magic point in time, the spring of 1946, when his old ally *Fortune* magazine ran a huge article on what was happening at the Beech Aircraft factory in Wichita, talking of national production rates of 250,000 units a year and vast export possibilities, Richard Buckminster Fuller really must have looked like a second Henry Ford. Another mighty industry, it seemed, was about to leap from the stone age into the air age with its own version of the price-chopping Model-T. Housing had broken through the craft-barrier into machine production. Not surprisingly, photographs of Fuller at that time show a powerful, confident figure, a giant of industry, a man on the brink of almost inconceivable achievement and influence. But it was not to be. The thousands of aircraft factory workers and the millions of hopeful purchasers world wide were destined to be disappointed, and Fuller himself was destined to suffer his second company liquidation in 20 years. This time it was not his father-in-law who pulled the plug on him by selling shares, nor a takeover company that elbowed him out. It was his fanatical determination to

Final construction task is hoisting into place of huge 5.5 metre rotating ventilator, as big as an entire DDU. This is done using the truck hoist.

Wind tunnel tested aerodynamic ventilator rides on Cadillac automobile wheel bearing at top of erection mast *(left)*. Finished house *(below)* is shown with stainless steel returnable packing cylinder capable of holding all components and fitting into the fuselage of a DC-6 transport plane.

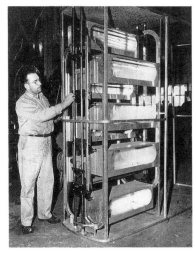

Interior picture shows spacious 8.5 metre diagonal living room with double perspex glazing. Smooth partition surfaces conceal motorized 'ovolving' paternoster shelves (right).

retain complete personal control of the project and refine the house still further before putting it into production that brought disaster.

The seeds of the final collapse of the company surfaced very early on when the $10 shares were first traded on the open market. Their value doubled within days and William Wasserman, a Philadelphia business associate of Wolf the publicity expert, bought 1,000 shares and joined the board. Because of his financial expertise Wasserman was soon made chairman and began to develop a financial plan. Wasserman intended to raise the $10 million that the Beech production engineers estimated would be necessary to tool up for production at the rate of 1,000 house kits a week. His proposed method was the issue of 750,000 new $1 shares that would be offered to the existing stock holders at a ratio of 10:1. The unclaimed 595,000 shares would then be sold for $5.95 million and the balance would be raised through bond issues or loans.

Under this scheme Fuller's own 5,500 share holding would have leaped in value to half a million dollars and it was expected by everyone that he would readily agree to it, but he did not. Throughout the spring and early summer of 1946 Wasserman and Fuller battled over the future of the company. According to Fuller's version of events plans for mass production were premature and several years of development were still needed before the 'Wichita' house could be marketed. 'If and when adequate time, money, resources and know-how have been invested in these houses', he had said grandly in 1944, 'they will be installable anywhere around the world at the same speed at which telephones can be installed'. At first this had sounded like understandable triumphalist hyperbole. Now, in 1946, with a proven mass market waiting and a large labour force growing impatient, it began to seem more like paranoia. The Wasserman faction rapidly came to believe that Fuller had developed a pathological resistance to letting the project move out of his personal day to day control, and was deliberately using his technical veto to prevent Wasserman from raising the necessary finance. Endlessly Fuller raised objections

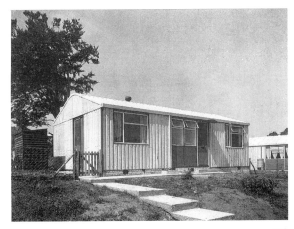

Sole surviving 'Wichita' house, subsequently insensitively converted into a summer cottage *(right)*, and contemporaneous British steel and asbestos 'ARCON' prefab *(below)*, contrast national approaches to war production 'reconversion'.

113

and defined new preparatory tasks. Before production started he insisted that special site preparation equipment be incorporated into the design of a special 'Dymaxion' delivery truck; that research be carried out into probable demarcation disputes between different construction unions; that the need for a training programme for specialist installers be explored...

Whatever the real reason for this behaviour, delay itself was rapidly becoming the enemy of the whole enterprise. Despite all the publicity there were still only two houses, one assembled and one in parts. Both had been made in a small annexe to the main Beechcraft plant, and both still belonged to the Army Air Corps. Nothing had been done to tool up for large scale production and all Beech Aircraft's military orders had been cancelled.

The final act of the drama began when Wasserman gave up, or appeared to, and offered to sell his shares back to Fuller and leave the company. Perhaps to his surprise Fuller accepted. Seeing the imminent collapse of a fantastic enterprise, Wolf flew to Anne Fuller's home on Long Island and told her that her husband had been having an affair with Cynthia Lacey ever since he had been in Kansas. Whether or not he expected Anne to help him put pressure on her husband is not clear, in any case she refused to believe him. Then Gaty followed in Wasserman's footsteps, selling the Beechcraft portion of the original shares back to Fuller as well. Within a week Richard Buckminster Fuller was the sole shareholder in a ruined business. No one had lost money, and no one had made money: but tragically no one had made 60,000 superbly designed prefabricated houses a year for the nation's veterans and the world's homeless either.

The only sequel to the epic tale of the 'Wichita' house concerns the fate of the two Air Corps prototypes. In the general collapse of the enterprise these were sold back to 'Fuller Houses Inc.' and then sold on liquidation to a local landowner. Using parts from the unbuilt second house he combined the two into a two-storey lakeside cottage standing on permanent foundations.

new department or school is a password, if not to extra funding, at least to a willing suspension of disbelief by sceptical administrators and a staying of the vengeful hand of orthodoxy. After all, Richard Buckminster Fuller invented the geodesic dome there.

Black Mountain came into existence because, in another Depression event that was to have incalculable consequences, a man named John Rice, unknown professor of classics at Rollins College in Florida and a former Rhodes Scholar, was sacked for recommending the abolition of the 'eight hour day' in favour of a more freewheeling approach to study. Luckily Rice had often discussed 'the ideal college' with his 'Athenian civilization class' so he and some Rollins faculty supporters took the opportunity to put his ideas into practice. They found a ready made campus to lease near Asheville, North Carolina and opened Black Mountain for business in the autumn of 1933. The keys to the new curriculum were democratic government and the central role of artistic studies, both of which remained important to the end. Black Mountain not only coincided with the New Deal in America, but with rise of Nazism and the fall of the Bauhaus in Europe. It benefited from both, being saved from conformity by New Deal radicalism, and from a lacklustre provincial faculty by an influx of Bauhaus refugees. The painter Josef Albers alone was enough to make its reputation and, to keep him, the school almost immediately broke its own taboo on permanent tenure. In 1940 faculty and students built a new campus to replace the rented one, and from then until Albers left and Gropius resigned as trustee the college offered basic courses in architecture as well as summer schools. In the summer of 1948, fresh from his catastrophe in Kansas, Albers' friend and confidante Richard Buckminster Fuller - unkindly described as 'a summer substitute for a legitimate architect' - was invited to teach a design class. Fuller had his students build a 15 metre geodesic hemisphere out of old venetian blinds, bolted together where they met at the intersections of 31 great circles: unfortunately it proved unable to support its own weight because the flattened strips flexed between

Thinking about thought.
Buckminster Fuller studies a
geometrical model in his
studio at Black Mountain
College in the summer of
1949. Above him to the left is
a dome model made from
venetian blind strips in the
previous year.

their triangularly intersecting joints. The structure was christened 'Supine Dome' and Fuller only retrieved his reputation that year by an epic thespian performance as Baron Medusa in the Black Mountain drama school production of Erik Satie's musical play *Le Piege de Meduse*, of which photographs still exist.

Undeterred by the first dome failure, in 1949 Albers recommended that Fuller be invited to direct the entire summer school programme. This was agreed by the faculty and Fuller, with some students from the Dearborn Street Institute of Design in Chicago where he had also been teaching, returned to North Carolina. One of the students who travelled with him was Don Richter, later to become president of Temcor, the Los Angeles company that 35 years later was to design and build the largest aluminium geodesic dome in the world, the 129 metre shell enclosing Howard Hughes' Spruce Goose flying boat.

'You succeed only when you stop failing', was Fuller's advice to the twelve resident students who signed up with him, for they had been made apprehensive by memories of the venetian blind fiasco. Not so Fuller, who afterwards maintained that the collapse had been intentional, designed to show students that 'the failure of structures is not necessarily hazardous'. This explanation is soberly recounted by Marks in *The Dymaxion World of Buckminster Fuller*.

In any case the 1949 summer school commenced work with another dome that Fuller brought with him in pieces. This structure was intended to enclose another Dearborn Street project called the 'autonomous living unit', a 7.5 m x 2.4 m x 2.4 m 'black box' in the form of a road container that could be unpacked into a completely equipped dwelling interior. The enclosing dome itself was made of short lengths of rigid aircraft duralumin tubing laced with cables. It assumed its proper shape when the cables were tightened up. Fuller had in fact already demonstrated this device to the Pentagon in Washington DC with a view to exploring its military potential as the nucleus of an air-transportable lightweight shelter system. At Black Mountain he and his students tested double inflatable

The plastic-skinned 'autonomous living unit' *(above)* erected at Black Mountain in 1949, and the unpacked contents of the 'black box' that fitted inside it.

plastic skins over it for waterproofing and insulation.

The only new dome project Fuller actually initiated at Black Mountain in the summer of 1949 necessitated the casting of triangular fibre glass sections. To complicate matters each triangular section was designed with a compound curvature for increased strength, and the curves were to be assembled in an alternately convex, concave pattern. Plaster moulds were made and then filled with chopped fibreglass bonded with resin. As it turned out the summer was so humid - or the application of hardening agents so unscientific - that the components would not set. Eventually they were abandoned and thrown into a ravine.

In the end the most promising work of the session was initiated by a student named Kenneth Snelson who had worked with Fuller the previous year. Snelson started out by making small moving sculptures whose compression members were discontinuous, being separated by tension wires. Fuller immediately recognised the structural potential of this arrangement and later appropriated it for himself, finally causing a rift with Snelson after the construction of a tall discontinuous compression mast at North Carolina State College in 1950. Fuller later gave the name 'tensegrity' to structures like this in which the compression members were not contiguous, and this is the term which is now generally used to describe them. The 'Skylon' that dominated the Festival of Britain site in 1951 was a tensegrity structure.

Disputes over authorship and Dearborn hangovers aside, by the end of Fullers' last year at Black Mountain the geodesic dome, which was soon to become his one great production success, had already crystallized into something like its final form. But only just in time: Charles Burchard, a Black Mountain professor, recalled in 1971 that, when Fuller was first invited to North Carolina in 1948, he was 'living a hand to mouth existence, thankful for room and board for the summer, a modest salary, and an opportunity to work in a sympathetic community of artists and friends'.

Indeed the former tycoon's route from collapsed prefabricated housing ventures to three-dimensional geometry had passed through a vale of trauma not totally dissimilar to the year of silence twenty years before. On his shamefaced return to New York from Wichita in 1946, Fuller had shunned publicity - all of it negative at that time, as might be supposed following the high hopes invested in the 'Wichita' house - and concentrated instead on reintegrating himself into family life and exploring a personal programme of meditation. His object in the latter enterprise was to make himself effective by disciplining his way of thinking so as to exclude all irrelevant matters. He wanted to train his brain so that his thoughts could emerge and develop with the utmost clarity before being clouded by second order objections. His sole apparent means of support while carrying out this self-schooling was his part-time teaching at the Dearborn Street Institute of Design and Black Mountain College.

The brilliant manner in which Fuller fused the development of a revolutionary structural system, the geodesic dome, out of a combination of many hundreds of paper and cardboard geometrical models that were ostensibly intended to be analogical aids for a system of thought, deserves careful consideration. Perhaps the best explanation of it is offered by his 1989 biographer Lloyd Steven Sieden.

'Thinking is sorting experiences', writes Sieden at the beginning of his exposition of Fuller's approach. 'Separating the huge set of experiences that are irrelevant from the very small set of experiences that are relevant.' But irrelevant material itself falls into two categories, and Fuller believed that imagining thought as a transparent sphere helped him to see a way of distinguishing between them. He visualized a situation in which all irrelevant experiences that were too small and too frequently occurring were inside the imaginary sphere, and all those that were too large and too infrequently occurring could be regarded as outside it.

The way Fuller imagined the thinking process, the surface of the imaginary sphere itself would then only consist of relevant experiences, or thoughts. He then wondered how many relevant experiences it would take to establish the 'insideness' and 'outsideness' necessary to create a sphere of thoughts. His answer was that while any two experiences could be joined by a line, it took three to fix their relationship - a concept perhaps not dissimilar to the journalistic principle that it takes three events to make a trend. This point Fuller diagrammatized by drawing a triangle. But to establish a sphere containing 'insideness' and 'outsideness', something robust enough to be called a thought, was impossible using flat triangles on paper, because the triangle had no integral space-enclosing depth. Three-dimensional structure, in thought as in geometry, could only be achieved by plotting in a fourth experience. The resultant three-dimensional model, a three-sided pyramid, or tetrahedron, Fuller came to believe, was the true geometrical model of a thought. It consisted of four points, or experiences, which in turn generated six sides, or relationships.

As Sieden summarised the process: 'When a person's mind uncovers comparable characteristics within two or three experiences, those experiences are subconsciously grouped together for further study. However, when a fourth experience with similar qualities is discovered and added to the others, the minimum number of items is discovered that has the potential of becoming a thought. In other words, with four experiences, the mind has enough information to produce a thought - a dividing structure the geometrical equivalent of which is a tetrahedron with four points.'

Structures, like theories, Fuller believed, could be made from collections of such self-supporting tetrahedrons and, because the three dimensional geometrical pattern these collections of tetrahedrons made when tessellated was spherical, they could be visualized as creating a mental 'insideness' and 'outsideness' in the same way as a physical structure of tetrahedrons could separate an 'interior' from an 'exterior'. The invisible sphere of the imagination could thus become a real sphere, and not just an analogy for one. Long before his sojourn at Black Mountain, Fuller had converted the *Bauhaus* epigram 'Less is more' into its 'Dymaxion' derivative 'More for less'. Now, by using the imaginary structure of thought visualized through a

The automated cotton mill project of 1950. This ambitious scheme, developed by Fuller while he was teaching at North Carolina State College, embodied not only a large geodesic structure, but space-frame truss cantilevered floors that were later to be patented and adapted for the Ford Rotunda.

geometrical analógy, he had seen a way to construct the type of 'minimum structure/maximum volume' enclosure that he believed was necessary to defeat the old economy of scarcity and exploitation in the real world.

Characteristically he set about creating a new corporate structure to handle this invention, but this time he contrived to avoid the conflict between raising investment capital and losing personal control that had brought down 'Fuller Houses Inc.'.

Since 'Fuller Houses Inc.' had ceased to exist in 1946 and only the moribund 'Fuller Research Foundation' founded at the same time remained, Fuller now had to launch a new business if he was to exploit the potential of the dome. His first move in 1949, while the dome concept had realized no more than the dubious 14.5 m diameter Black Mountain enclosure, was to formed a private company called 'Geodesics Inc.', with himself as president and registered offices at the Fuller family home where Anne and Allegra lived in Forest Hills, New York.

'Geodesics Inc.' had not long to wait before it found customers. Perhaps because Fuller had not lost all his wartime Washington military contacts, when he moved from Black Mountain to North Carolina State College in 1950 to develop the '90 per cent Automatic Cotton Mill' project, 'Geodesics Inc.' was already extending feelers in the direction of the United States Air Force and the Marine Corps for the provision of 'skybreak' shelter domes for military stores, and transportable plastic dome hangars for jet fighters.

The Cotton Mill, with its eight cantilevered floors of automated and vertically stacked machinery enclosed by a transparent 70 per cent dome, was financed by local Southern interests, but it never progressed beyond maquette stage. Later its space-frame flooring system was to be patented by the inventor under the name 'Octet Truss'. But in 1950 other possibilities had emerged. Buckminster Fuller, the former failed entrepreneur, was now much in demand as a visionary professor and technical consultant. In 1951 he left North Carolina State and moved to the prestigious Massachusetts Institute of Technology. There his students worked on various developmental projects including wooden geodesics; a 20 metre diameter 'Skybreak' dome for an auditorium in Aspen, Colorado; a series of smaller 'Skybreaks' for military and domestic use, and the Marine Corps hangar project. For the last they developed foamed polystyrene, tubular aluminium and glass fibre dome variants with wide sliding or curved bascule doors. The success of these projects led to an association with the Marine Corps that was to fund Fuller's dome developments for several years.

It was while he was at MIT that Fuller filed the most important patent application of his life. On December 12th 1951 he submitted a report to the United States patent office on the geodesic dome that showed how far he had been able to concretize what had merely started out as thinking about thought. 'My invention', he wrote modestly, 'relates to a framework for enclosing space. A good index to the performance of any building frame is the structural weight required to shelter a square foot of floor from the weather. In conventional wall and roof designs the figure is often 2500 kg per square metre. I have discovered how to do the job at around 4 kg per square metre by constructing a frame of generally spherical form in which the main structural elements are interconnected in a geodesic pattern of approximately great circle arcs intersecting to form a three-way grid, and covering or lining this frame with a skin of plastic material'. This basic patent was granted in the United States on June 29th 1954 and Fuller received royalties on all the geodesic domes built under it until it expired seventeen years later. While most of these domes were relatively small structures designed to shelter humans or equipment in adverse conditions in the Arctic, the Antarctic or on top of mountains, some of them were of extraordinary size and importance, perhaps the most prestigious being the United States Pavilion at the Montreal Expo of

The early geodesic domes were developed at universities, as student projects, or for the military, principally the United States Marine Corps. Fuller's work for universities soon encompassed most of North America. In 1951 this aluminium tube structure supporting an internal envelope *(above)* was erected in Montreal. A foldable diamond honeycomb paperboard geodesic *(left)* followed in 1952 and led to cardboard kit domes.

An aluminium foil-clad version of one of the cardboard domes *(right)* was erected in Montreal by McGill University students and survived the Canadian winter of 1957 unharmed *(below)*.

Two-frequency structures made from sheet materials were also erected. This 'Plydome' *(left)* was assembled in des Moines, Iowa, and a corrugated steel version with plastic windows *(below)* was erected at the University of Natal in South Africa.

Later cardboard domes were used by the Peace Corps overseas. Fuller *(right)* inspects a prototype Peace Corps dome in 1961. A final version of the 'Plydome' was the 'Pine Cone', a 14 metre 'shingled' dome using uncut plywood sheets that was erected at Cornell University *(below)*.

1967, a gigantic acrylic-glazed geodesic sphere designed by Buckminster Fuller in association with Shoji Sadao, his collaborator for the last thirty-two years of his life.

Shoji Sadao, who was of Japanese extraction but born and raised in Los Angeles, was destined to exert a powerful practical influence on Fuller, especially during the era of the giant projects which is discussed in the next chapter. He was trained as an architect at Cornell University and was a student there when he met Buckminster Fuller for the first time in May 1952. Fuller was then a visiting professor, supervising the construction of a 6 metre diameter 'Miniature Earth' which was to be mounted on the roof of a university building and oriented in such a way that its north-south polar axis exactly paralleled the true axis of the earth. The difference in displacement between the real earth's and the Miniature Earth's centres was negligible and, with the eye of the observer at the center of the Miniature Earth, the view out into planetary space through the 'conti-

His student at the time of the Miniature Earth project was Shoji Sadao, later his collaborator for 30 years. Sadao is third from the left in this 1961 photograph of Fuller in Japan. Fuller is in the centre of the picture with Anne to his right.

nents' - added as translucent mesh screens - was identical to the view that would have been seen from that point on the earth's surface.

The modest Cornell sphere was a psychologically effective planetarium that had a profound effect upon Fuller's thinking thereafter. When it had been dismantled he employed Sadao to help him realize a new version of the 1943 'Dymaxion Air-Ocean World Map' which he had patented in 1946. The new version was published in 1954 and is still in print. In the same year Fuller and Sadao formed a second dome company, 'Synergetics Inc.' with offices in Raleigh, North Carolina.

In 1955, working with students from the University of Minnesota, Fuller and Sadao pursued the possibilities opened up by the Cornell sphere by putting forward a proposal for a 122 metre diameter 'Miniature Earth' to be sited opposite the United Nations building on the banks of the east River in New York. If carried out, this project would have presented a model earth's surface so large that individual houses would have been visible. The idea of the gigantic 'Miniature Earth' was to surface again during Fuller's life. He never lost sight of the educational potential of what he called the 'social navigational' use of the giant geodesic sphere, sometimes as a solid object, and sometimes as an enclosure containing a 'geoscope' representing in animated form such phenomena as the rate of increase of the world's population or the consumption of resources. Gigantic domes and spheres of instruction of this kind also fed into the series of immense engineering projects that he and Sadao proposed during the 1960s.

But in 1954 large applications of the geodesic principle were still some distance away. In that year Fuller and Sadao were working at a smaller scale and with humbler materials. In the civilian realm they successfully perfected a system of perforated paperboard dome construction, with which 'Geodesics Inc.' built an 11 metre diameter dome and a 22 metre prize-winning dome for the Milan Triennale. On the military front 1954 also saw the design and successful testing of a series of magnesium-framed, dacron-clad, air-transportable helicopter hangars for the Marine Corps, the largest of which were designed to be carried in two superimposable sections. Derivatives of these Marine Corps flying hangars included inflatable 'air beam' domes that could be erected by compressed air in seconds, and pre-assembled shelter domes that could be air-lifted from aircraft carriers. The most sophisticated Marine Corps prototype was for a 15 metre dome whose frame was self-erecting, using gas powered, self-erecting frameworks with piston-deployed magnesium ball-jointed tripod structural frames that could be animated at the pull of a lanyard. This device was developed with the aid of graduate students at Washington University, Saint Louis.

The final report on Fuller's Marine Corps studies published in 1959 described his range of air-transportable domes as 'the first basic improvement in mobile military shelters in the past 2,600 years'. Only 3 per cent of the weight of traditional tents and hutments, they required 6 per cent of the packing volume, 14 per cent of the cost, and only 1 per cent of the erection time. Total estimated savings from the universal use of geodesic shelters by the Marine Corps in the field were put at $45 million.

Radomes for the Army and the Air Force proved an important market for Fuller's geodesics. Often sited at high altitude and in inaccessible regions, the standard structure he proposed was a 17 metre diameter 75 per cent non-metallic sphere made from diamond-shaped fibre glass components that could be delivered by helicopter in kit form to the most difficult locations and erected in 14 hours. In use since 1956 many of these structures are still in service.

Important as these military projects were in providing capital for research and development during the early years of Fuller's dome explorations, none of them was of long term importance in terms of public acceptance of the dome as an architectural form. The commission that achieved this goal almost single handed was the Ford Rotunda roof dome, a 28 metre circular space frame designed to enclose an open lightwell at

The domes for the US Marine Corps were the most impressive developed in the 1950s. The Marine Corps concept was of a completely helicopter-transportable hangar and storage capability achieved by dome structures, as shown in this artist's impression. At the opposite extreme this lanyard-triggered air-beam inflatable *(below)* is typical of the instant deployment capability that was required at a smaller scale.

Later magnesium framed fabric storage domes could be erected by untrained personnel in two hours, carried by ten men *(left)* and could withstand simulated 120 mph winds. Sequence *(below & this page)* shows storage dome being brought by helicopter from carrier flight deck to shore. Figure standing next to flight deck lift is Buckminster Fuller.

Radomes too led to rapid developments in lightness and fast assembly. First fibre glass frame *(left)* soon gave place to the first prototype 16.5 metre polyester fibre glass radome *(below)*, seen here under construction on Long Island, and at night after completion *(right)*.

First production 16.5 metre radome was built at the Bell Laboratories, Whippany, New Jersey *(below)*.

the centre of the Ford Motor Company's courtesy building in Dearborn, Michigan. Glazing supported by conventional steelwork would have weighed more than the inner walls of the building could support, but Fuller's aluminium and polystyrene dome effortlessly spanned the void at an all-up weight of only 4.25 tonnes. The dome itself was in reality a spherical truss in which triangular aluminium frame sub-assemblies were combined into fifteen tetrahedra, each constituting a large triangular element. These self-supporting elements were then combined into a circular shell and their outer surface glazed with transparent polystyrene panels, whose crystalline effect produced astonishing photographic results when the work was finished. The construction of this dome represented the first important commercial sponsorship of the geodesic principle and the beginning of large scale use of domes for space enclosure by American business. From the Ford dome onwards interest spread to large clear-spanning multifunctional structures like the demountable 30 metre and 60 metre exhibition domes with their suspended synthetic fabric envelopes that were used by the United States Information Service overseas. These could be erected repeatedly and delivered in single aircraft. They could be put up and taken down by unskilled local labour in 48 hours. Like the radomes, these exhibition domes too were produced by Fuller's wholly owned companies 'Geodesics Inc.' and 'Synergetics Inc.'

By the end of the 1950s the user of the largest geodesic domes in the world was the Union Tank Car Company, a railroad car manufacturer. In Baton Rouge, Louisiana, in 1958 the company built a 116 metre aluminium dome to enclose its repair facilities - at the time the largest clear-span enclosure anywhere in the world. This giant was followed a year later by a slightly smaller 108 metre dome of similar design erected at Wood River, Illinois. This dome was the first to be assembled on the ground and raised into position using pneumatic jacks. At the very end of the decade the American Society for Metals saluted the arrival of lightweight dome engineering by erecting a 76 metre openwork double aluminium dome over its new Cleveland

The Ford Rotunda dome of 1953 was the watershed in dome developments for architecture. Designed to enclose the courtyard of the main Ford building in Dearborn, Michigan *(right)*, it spanned 28 metres with a weight of only 4.25 tonnes using 'Octet' trusses developed from the floors of the earlier cotton mill project. Fuller holds Ford dome model *(below)*, showing how it is composed of fifteen prefabricated aluminium tetrahedra.

139

Fabricating aluminium triangles for the Ford Rotunda Dome *(left)* and junction of space-frame dome and existing parapet *(below)* show size of components.

headquarters designed by architect John Kelly.

While the development of larger span domes and related structures proceeded apace, Buckminster Fuller continued to explore new possibilities with students in schools of architecture all over the world. At the university of Natal in South Africa he and his students developed a 5.5 metre corrugated aluminium dome dwelling with a hardwood and polyethylene floor that could be produced at a material cost of only $150. In Des Moines, Iowa, a two-frequency geodesic plywood dome was constructed that was later adapted into a chapel in Korea, and as the prototype for a low-cost garage unit. At McGill University in Montreal, an aluminium-foil clad paperboard dome was erected that proved capable of withstanding a Canadian winter.

By 1960 the Pease Woodwork Company of Ohio had put a standard geodesic dome-house into production. This 12 metre plywood-clad icosahedral structure was framed in timber and conventionally glazed, making it less remarkable in appearance than Fuller's own early 'Skybreak dwelling' exercises of 1952. Nonetheless when Fuller accepted a professorship at the University of Southern Illinois in 1968 he purchased a Pease dome and made it his family home for several years. At the time of Fuller's death the English architect Norman Foster was in the process of designing a more sophisticated transparent double rotatable dome house for the Fuller family, but of this project only drawings and a model remain.

Between the unsuccessful 'Supine Dome' of 1949 and the huge, column-free space-enclosing structures for the Union Tank Car Company, a bare ten years had elapsed. In that time Fuller's reputation had shed the eccentric and dubious overtones it had accumulated in the preceding 20 years and he had begun to be the recipient of a shower of honours that was to continue to descend upon him in an unending stream until his death.

This process began with a major exhibition of his work at the New York Museum of Modern Art in 1959 for which a tall 'Tensegrity' mast was erected in the museum's sculpture garden. Indoors, ultra-lightweight

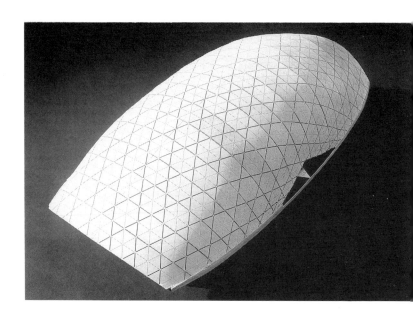

continuous tension/discontinuous compression domes
were erected in which every component was identical,
showing that Fuller had broken through into spheroi-
dal systems using unitary modular denominators for
the first time. Five years later with the development
of the Monohex Geodesic, better known as the 'Fly's
Eye' dome, he was able to achieve the same single-
component inventory for sheet materials such as
aluminium, steel and glass fibre that could be used for
low-cost housing.

Throughout this period of massive growth in the
national and international use of geodesic structures,
Fuller himself continued to live and work as the comprehensive design philosopher and sage he had become

The largest geodesic dome structures erected in the 1950s were the all-steel Union Tank Car domes at Baton Rouge, Louisiana, which spanned 116 metres *(left)*, and at Wood River, Illinois. The second dome was raised using pneumatic jacks as picture on right shows. Another large dome, notable because it was fabricated in two skins without cladding, was the 75 metre American Society for Metals dome *(below, right)* erected in Cleveland, Ohio, in 1959.

145

in the years following the 'Wichita' debacle. Between 1955 and the end of his life he circumnavigated the world 57 times in connection with lectures and consultancies. In 1958, at the age of 63, he was invited to London to deliver the annual discourse to the Royal Institute of British Architects. He returned in 1962 to open an exhibition of his work at the United States Embassy and on that occasion presented a spherical geodesic chandelier, designed and built by James and Gill Meller, to HRH Princess Margaret and her designer husband Anthony Armstrong Jones. At the time of Fuller's death this memento was still in use at Kensington Palace. Subsequently Fuller was honoured by the American Institute of Architects and successive American presidents, in addition to other national leaders. But of all the honours heaped upon Fuller in his declining years, none was to equal the posthumous christening of a virtually indestructible carbon atom with his name. In 1985 Dr Harry Kroto, Dr Robert Curl, Dr Richard Smalley and their students at Rice University in Texas identified the smallest atoms of carbon in soot as consisting of truncated icosahedrons, the pattern of hexagons and pentagons made familiar by the shape of the geodesic dome, and the closest-fitting planar shape that can be drawn upon a spherical surface. Noting that this extremely strong arrangement of one of the earth's most common substances probably occurs even in the gas clouds between the stars, the professors dubbed the atoms 'Buckminsterfullerenes'.

the giant projects

'Architecture is voodoo. The architects don't initiate anything; they just go to work when the client says so. They know how to draw, but they don't know how to design an airplane. They don't go to Douglas and say tell me what you've found out today about the tensile strength of that new steel or aluminium. They have approximately nothing to do with evolution. I think the younger architects may be changing, I think they understand what I'm saying.'

Richard Buckminster Fuller
New York Times 23 April 1967

'Tensegrity', as we have seen, was the name Buckminster Fuller gave to the continuous tension/discontinuous compression structural system that he developed from the articulated sculptures of Kenneth Snelson at Black Mountain College in 1949. Over the years, starting with the construction of masts using more than one type of preformed compression strut component, and then moving on to spheres and domes, Fuller progressively refined and simplified his tensegrity structures until in 1959 at the University of Oregon he and his students built the first unitary component tensegrity sphere. The wafer-thin structural depth and lightness of this framework offered him, for the first time in the geodesic era, another approach to the fundamental weight-to-volume problem he had first tackled in '*4-D*' thirty years before. At that time Fuller had boasted that the 230 metre rigid airship *Graf Zeppelin* should be seen as a source of architectural inspiration, a 60-storey skyscraper on its side. This time, on August 31st 1959, he applied for a United States patent covering all tensile-integrity structures. The patent was granted in November 1962.

The preamble to this patent application makes clear that, for Buckminster Fuller, the invention of lightweight tensegrity construction had cleared away the last obstacle to space-enclosing projects of enormous size. At his New York Museum of Modern Art exhibition held in the same year as the construction of the Oregon dome, Fuller had showed a second room-sized tensegrity sphere made entirely of ultra-light aluminium alloy tubes and stretch-resistant aircraft control wires. Visitors marvelled at its strength and lightness but few appreciated its importance. Working from it Fuller had calculated the load factors for much larger tensegrity structures and he knew that from now on the sky was literally the limit.

The primary structural element of the unitary component tensegrity sphere exhibited at the Museum of Modern Art resembled nothing so much as an optical illusion. It consisted of three rigid compression members in the shape of a triangle, with each member passing over one end of one of the adjoining members, and under one end of the next without actually touching. The three compression members, and all the other triangles of members that went to make up the sphere, were held in place, by an endless net of tension 'turbining about phantom hubs', as Fuller himself described it. His purpose in creating this structural system was, he wrote in the lucid language of the patent application, 'to bring the slenderness, lightness and strength of the suspension bridge cable into the realm previously dominated by the compression column concept of building'.

What Fuller had satisfied himself about by calculation in relation to the structural weight per unit area enclosed by tensegrity structures would have made a lesser man shrug his shoulders and turn his mind to something else. Because of the enormous efficiency of tension as opposed to compression, and the great predominance of tensile structuring in his tensegrity spheres, Fuller had discovered that there was no reason why tensegrity domes of over 3 kilometres in diameter could not could be built using state of the art aircraft industry materials and methods.

He had gone into the question further. Based on his experience with the Ford Rotunda and other large domes already built using much heavier jointing technologies, Fuller was able to predict that such huge tensegrity domes could be assembled in segments and, again because of their extraordinary lightness, the segments could be flown into their assembly positions using helicopters. An entire 3 kilometre dome, he calculated, would only weigh 4,000 tonnes.

'A fleet of sixteen of the large Sikorsky helicopters could fly all the segments into position for a 1.6 kilometre high, 3 kilometre wide dome in three months at a cost of $200 million,' he wrote in 1960. 'A dome of this size would cover New York City, east and west, from the East River to the Hudson, at 42nd Street, and north and south, from 62nd street to 22nd street - an area of fifty blocks which includes all of the upper Manhattan skyscraper city. A dome of this kind would prevent snow and rain from falling on the protected area and control the effects of sunlight and the quality of the air. Since all the New York Steam Company and Edison Company plants which supply this area are outside the circle, the buildings within the dome could be heated and still exclude the primary fumes which now pollute the area.'

Fuller went on to explain that only electrically powered vehicles would be permitted in the covered zone. His descriptions of the project were reported and translated all over the world with amazement and disbelief, but he turned his attention to the structural details as though the project were simply a work of architecture. Not only would the depth of structure needed for the dome be sufficient, he said, to make it possible for housing projects to be constructed to great

The first unitary component tensegrity sphere constructed at the University of Oregon *(left)*. This was the development that 'cleared the way to space-enclosing projects of enormous size'. The first of these to be proposed had in fact been a giant 'octet' truss hangar for the Boeing B-36 bomber *(below, right)*, for which a patent had been filed in 1956, but the development of tensegrity structures created far more elegant possibilities.

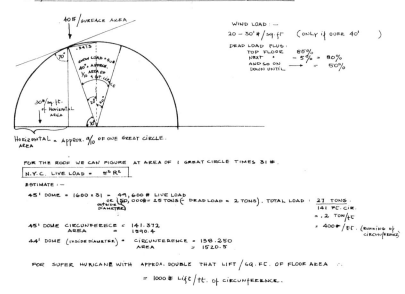

FACTORS of STRESS CALCULATIONS OF STRUCTURE FOR NEW YORK CITY.

40# / SURFACE AREA

.3413

70°

SNOW LOAD + 40#
40# APPROX.
1/10 AREA OF
1 GT. CIRCLE

30#/sq. ft.
of HORIZONTAL
AREA

20°

10°

WIND LOAD : —
20 – 30' #/sq. ft   (ONLY if OVER 40'   )

DEAD LOAD PLUS :
TOP FLOOR   85%
NEXT   "   – 5% = 80%
AND SO ON
DOWN UNTIL ⟶   = 50%

HORIZONTAL = APPROX. 9/10 OF ONE GREAT CIRCLE.
AREA

FOR THE ROOF WE CAN FIGURE AT AREA OF 1 GREAT CIRCLE TIMES 31 #.

N.Y.C. LIVE LOAD = $\pi^2 R^2$

ESTIMATE : —

45' DOME = 1600 × 31 = 49,600 # LIVE LOAD
OR (50,000# = 25 TONS (– DEAD LOAD = 2 TONS). TOTAL LOAD : 27 TONS.
OUTSIDE   141 FT. CIR.
DIAMETER)   = .2 TON/ft

45' DOME CIRCUMFERENCE = 141.372
        AREA   = 1590.4

44' DOME (INSIDE DIAMETER) = CIRCUMFERENCE = 138.250
                              AREA   = 1520.5

= 400# /FT. (RUNNING of
                  CIRCUMFERENCE)

FOR SUPER HURICANE WITH APPROX. DOUBLE THAT LIFT / SQ. FT. OF FLOOR AREA ∴

= 1000 # LIFT/FT. OF CIRCUMFERENCE.

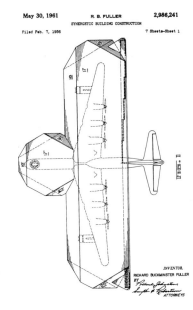

May 30, 1961   R. B. FULLER   2,986,241
SYNERGETIC BUILDING CONSTRUCTION

Filed Feb. 7, 1956   7 Sheets—Sheet 1

INVENTOR.
RICHARD BUCKMINSTER FULLER
BY
ATTORNEYS

Within a year of the construction of the Oregon sphere Fuller, with a set of calculations as famous as Einstein's theory of relativity *(left)*, had confirmed the feasibility of a tensegrity dome large enough to cover fifty blocks of Manhattan Island. He and Sadao designed it and published a photomontage of the projected 3.2 kilometre structure *(above)*, intended to be assembled by a fleet of helicopters in six months. The project is still published as a novelty to this day.

heights within its envelope, but - on February 8th 1962 in a London lecture given by Fuller on the subject reprinted in the magazine *New Scientist* - he drew attention to an aerial photomontage of the project in which the microscopic shape of the ocean liner *Queen Mary* was arrowed in dock in the East River.

'The thickness of the structural members of the New York tensegrity dome would be about the thickness of the masts of the *Queen Mary*,' he explained. 'In that picture *Queen Mary* is in harbour and you can see her clearly enough, but you cannot see her masts; therefore you could not see the structural components of the enclosing dome. The dome is invisible - just as invisible as a fly-screen when you get quite far away from it.'

Clearly something dramatic had happened to Richard Buckminster Fuller's thinking between the failure of the 'Supine Dome' at Black Mountain and the triumphant success of the Oregon tensegrity sphere. The fragment of the transcript of his lecture quoted above is nothing less than a literal description of the process he was later to immortalize as 'ephemeralization', whereby doing more for less can lead to an implosion of functions, one into another, until only a gossamer thin but steely strong multifunctional envelope takes the place of the separate 'cultures' of architecture, building and aesthetics.

Considering in retrospect the decade of rapid development that the invention of the geodesic dome had brought about, it is clear that the greatest single impact of the event upon him cannot have been simply 'success' - in the conventional sense of wealth and celebrity. The impact was something altogether more awe-inspiring and unprecedented. It was that, for the first time since he left the Navy in 1922, Fuller had witnessed limitless resources and power in action. Not only that, but these resources had been placed at his disposal. He had tasted the power of science and technology allied to the authority of giant organizations like the Marine Corps, the United States Air Force, the Ford Motor Company and other lesser corporations. More importantly still he had seen what such power, properly directed, might do for mankind.

In the years since 1950 Fuller had watched with admirals while aircraft carriers were ordered about simply to demonstrate the helicopter launching of geodesic domes into the air; he had stood with generals while tethered twin engined aircraft ran their fuel tanks dry in attempts to simulate the effect of hurricane winds on tiny geodesic igloos; he had witnessed the entire might of the United States armed services summoned to act as one single enthusiastic audience for the performance of his most insignificant inventions. And this experience had made him both wiser and more indignant. It had made him see once again the huge world of human possibilities that lay beyond the stunted thinking of governments, construction companies, and what he termed the 'voodoo' of closed professions.

In the first spectacular decade of the dome, Fuller had travelled the globe and felt the far-flung concentration of United States national power that had defeated the Germans and the Japanese only a few years before. When he expressed opinions about the future of design and construction after that, he thought about it on a new scale. He had a new name for it, he called it 'Design Science'. As early as 1961 he had conceived a 100 acre dome project, intended to enclose an entire sports complex complete with a racecourse. The cause may have been ignoble but the scale was right. If architecture and building were to keep pace with what advanced military technology could now do - and global survival now required - then a massive increase in the scale of environmental thinking was essential. In 1962 at the age of 67 he told an audience of student architects in London:

'Form is *not* following function, if we are using 'high-priority' technology. We have been misinforming ourselves in thinking that what we call 'modern' is really a highly advanced technical capability... With the development of rocketry, and when the *Sputnik* went in the sky, the aeroplane was made suddenly obsolete as the great weapon of man, and with it its enormous supporting technology and production capacity. So the production capabilities that were very scarce yesterday, are suddenly ours in great abundance. In fact we have an excess of such capability on both sides of the Iron Curtain today. It is that excess in production and design capability that I am now proposing architects and architecture students around the world should use in the development of structures for the forward development of man.'

It was this line of thought that was to lead Fuller to make one of his most quoted observations a few years later; 'The answer to the housing problem lies on the way to the moon'.

That this view of the limitless social and economic possibilities of truly advanced technology was not an isolated one at the time is attested by the proliferation of 'megastructure' architectural and engineering projects that appeared during the 1960s, many of them still under consideration for execution to this day. Vast irrigation projects for Africa and the Middle East; reverse flow river projects in the Soviet Union, and huge schemes for the reorganization of cities using massive prefabricated housing complexes and multiple-level transport interchanges were published throughout the decade. The engineer Zoltan Makowski wrote in 1966 in a special issue of the magazine *Architectural Design* devoted to three-dimensional structures:

'We are on the eve of a great architectural revolution, marking a change-over from the two-dimensional structures of the past to the three-dimensional occupiable space systems of the future. The advent of the electronic computer has made it possible for the first time in the history of civil engineering to tackle these complex structural analyses... The ever increasing number of steel and aluminium space structures built all over the world clearly indicates that the momentum of this development is growing... Space structures are not a passing fashion.'

Fuller himself spelled out prophetically what this 'revolution' might mean for the architectural profession in the pages of *Architectural Forum* in the same year, when he wrote:

'Architecture as practised today is a slave function, exercising good taste in purchasing and assembling industrially available components, a superficial veil to cover the steel or concrete frames that are completely conventionalized and organized by engineers. This slave profession only goes to work when it is hired and told what to do... Under such conditions all you can do is arrange a few brick panels between the columns. That world of architecture is going out. From now on there are going to be new individuals who do not just assume that a client knows what he wants, or a society knows what it wants to do. These individuals are going to examine environmental controls, human needs, world resources and industry's capabilities before they design anything.'

From 1960 onwards, Fuller and Sadao strove with extraordinary daring to demonstrate what such 'new individuals' might do to hasten the advent of an ephemeralized space-structure architecture of the future. They worked at two levels, from the practical level of construction for real corporate or national clients, to the visionary or utopian projects they proposed because they were possible and valuable, even if no human political or commercial organization could at that time summon the resolution to execute them.

Apart from the Manhattan dome, the project that grew most directly from Fuller's first shattering calculations about the limitless space-enclosing potential of tensegrity structures, was a buoyancy study based on earlier thinking about lighter than air craft. Fuller clearly conceived the idea of resuscitating giant airships like the *Graf Zeppelin* constructed according to the tensegrity principle in 1960 or 1961, but he abandoned the notion almost immediately. The power units and control mechanisms for such immense craft would be an unnecessarily complication. Better by far that even larger spheres should orbit the earth at high altitudes, carried by the winds like giant balloons. Fuller had worked out that a 30 metre tensegrity sphere weighing 1.5 tonnes would enclose 3.5 tonnes of air, Doubling the diameter of this sphere would raise the weight of the structure only to 3 tonnes but the weight of the enclosed air to 28 tonnes. By enlarging the sphere to nearly one kilometre in diameter, Fuller believed that

A one hundred foot diameter geodesic sphere weighing three tons encloses seven tons of air. The air to structural weight ratio is 2/1. When we double the size so that geodesic sphere is 200 feet in diameter the weight of the structure goes up to 7 tons while the weight of the air goes up to 56 tons -- the air to structure ratio changes to 8/1. When we double the size again to a 400 feet geodesic sphere -- the size of several geodesic domes now operating -- the weight of the air inside comes to about 500 tons while the weight of the structure goes up to 16 tons. Air weight to structure weight ratio is now 33/1. When we get to a geodesic sphere one-half mile in diameter, the weight of the air enclosed is so great that the weight of the structure itself becomes of relatively neg-

ligible magnitude for the ratio is 1,000/1. When the sun shines on an open frame aluminum geodesic sphere of one-half mile diameter the sun penetrating through the frame and reflected from the concave far side, bounces back into the sphere and gradually heats the interior atmosphere to a mild degree. When the interior temperature of the sphere rises only one degree Fahrenheit, the weight of air pushed out of the sphere is greater than the weight of the spherical frame geodesic structure. This means that the total weight of the interior air, plus the weight of the structure, is much less than the surrounding atmosphere. This means that the total assemblage, of the geodesic sphere and its contained air, will have to float outwardly, into the sky, being displaced

by the heavy atmosphere around it. When a great bank of mist lies in a valley in the morning and the sun shines upon it, the sun heats the air inside the bank of mist. The heated air expands and therefore pushes some of itself outside the mist bank. The total assembly of the mist bank weighs less than the atmosphere surrounding it and the mist bank floats aloft into the sky. Thus are clouds manufactured. As geodesic spheres get larger than one-half mile in diameter they become floatable cloud structures. If their surfaces were draped with outwardly hung polyethelene curtains to retard the rate at which air would come back in at night, the sphere and its internal atmosphere would continue to be so light as to remain aloft. Such sky- floating geodesic

spheres may be designed to float at preferred altitudes of thousands of feet. The weight of human beings added to such prefabricated 'cloud nines' would be relatively negligible. Many thousands of passengers could be housed aboard one mile diameter and larger cloud structures. The passengers could come and go from cloud to cloud, or cloud to ground, as the clouds float around the earth or are anchored to mountain tops. While the building of such floating clouds is several decades hence, we may foresee that along with the floating tetrahedronal cities, air-deliverable skyscrapers, submarine islands, sub-dry surface dwellings, domed-over cities, flyable dwelling machines, rentable, autonomous-living, black boxes, that man may be able to converge and deploy around earth without its depletion.

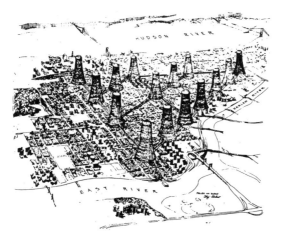

Fuller and Sadao's second giant project involving the new dome technology was a scheme for gigantic spheres called 'Cloud Structures' (above). These tensegrity structures, harking back to Fuller's early interest in lighter than air flight, were to be globes more than 1.6 metres in diameter that were intended to rise into the air as a result of the sun heating the air contained within them. Their structural self-weight would be so small that with a population of 'many thousands' they could float around the earth or anchor themselves to mountain tops. The 1964 successor to the 'Cloud Structures' was a large-scale urban renewal project for the New York district of Harlem (left).

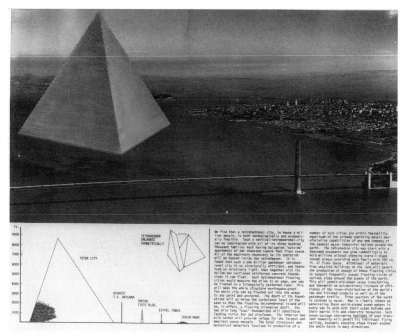

Housing 110,000 families in 100-storey hollow towers, Fuller and Sadao proposed to resurrect Fuller's '4-D' parking structure of 1928 and marry it to an urban megastructure linked at 10-storey height by suspension bridge motorways. Fuller and Sadao's concern with water-based urban centres came to the fore with a vast floating project called 'Tetrahedronal City' *(above)*. Triangular in plan form, with sides of 3.2 kilometres, this concrete megastructure rose to a peak 2.5 metres high in the sky. Various photomontages showed the project afloat in San Francisco Bay, in Tokyo Bay, and aground elsewhere in Japan. Floating versions incorporated deep-water harbours and jet aircraft landing strips. All were intended to accommodate one million persons.

the ratio of structural weight to enclosed air volume would become negligible and the warming effect of the sun upon the enclosed air would be sufficient to allow the sphere to rise like a cloud.

'Many thousands of passengers could be housed aboard 1.7 kilometre diameter and larger cloud structures', he told his biographer Robert Marks in 1962. 'The passengers could come and go from cloud to cloud, or cloud to ground, as the clouds float around the earth or are anchored to mountain tops. While the building of floating clouds is several decades hence. we may foresee that along with the floating tetrahedronal cities, air-deliverable skyscrapers, submarine islands, sub-dry surface dwellings. domed-over cities, flyable dwelling machines, rentable, autonomous-living, black boxes, that man may be able to converge and deploy around earth without its depletion'

157

Fuller and Sadao saw the solution to the global shelter problem as one goal of the massive application of formerly military technology to construction projects of an appropriate grandeur and daring. In 1964 the Manhattan dome and the 'Cloud Structures' were followed by another drastic project for New York. This was a proposal for the complete redevelopment of Harlem north of 110th street, rehousing 110,000 resident families in a series of fifteen vast 100-storey hollow, mast-supported towers joined ten storeys up by a network of motorway suspension bridges. The towers themselves were to have featured supermarkets and community facilities interleaved with decks containing five apartments per floor, all arranged within the thickness of the perimeter structure. A double helix of entrance and exit ramps for cars was to have been wrapped around their central masts to provide access to parking inside. This marked a rare reversion to one of Fuller's earliest ideas, the '4-D Tower Garage' that he proposed for the 1933 Chicago World's Fair. The Harlem project was designed to end congestion on the ground and allow for the gradual replacement of the existing street pattern and its eventual conversion to parks and recreational uses.

Better known than the Harlem slum-clearance project was Fuller's 1965 attempt to do for San Francisco Bay what the 3 kilometre dome and the Harlem redevelopment had done for Manhattan. 'Tetrahedronal City' was intended as a vast pyramidal floating atoll providing accomodation for one million persons within its triangular 3.2 kilometre-sided footprint. Each of its immense honeycomb concrete walls, rising to a 2,500 metre peak, was to have contained 5,000 apartments, each with 200 square metres of floorspace, internal and external balconies and spectacular views. The base of the atoll was to have contained an artificial harbour and a vast park, lit through broad 'city centre' openings every 50th floor. Shown moored in San Francisco bay, the earthquake-proof 'Tetrahedronal city' dwarfed its well-known surroundings. Fuller believed such enormous structures should not be isolated wonders, like the Eiffel tower, but produced in large numbers all over the world, as and where needed. Under the influence of his Japanese patron, the TV magnate Matsutaro Shoriki, he visualised a land-based Tetrahedronal City located outside Tokyo, and also another floating in Tokyo Bay, but most discussions of the project were centred on its marine potential. Because they were stable, buoyant and self-sufficient through solar power and wave-generated energy, Fuller proposed that Tetrahedronal Cities could be assembled and towed out to offshore anchorage points. Marks reports him saying later of the project:

'The total structural and mechanical materials involved in the production of a number of these (Tetrahedronal) cities are within feasibility magnitude of the already operating metals manufacturing capabilities of any one company of the several major industrial nations around the earth... Withdrawal of materials from obsolete buildings on the land will permit the production of enough of these floating cities to support mid-ocean cargo transferring and therewith an extraordinary increase of efficiency in world raw and finished material distribution.'

A later floating city concept that owed much to 'Tetrahedronal City' was 'Triton City', a far more prosaic and detailed study financed by the United States Department of Housing and Urban Development in 1968. 'Triton City' was the result of an attempt to explore the technical and economic feasibility of developing areas of sheltered water adjacent to the cores of major cities. Fuller and Sadao formed a separate organisation, 'Triton Foundation Inc', to carry out their analysis of the problems.

In its published form Triton City consisted of a complex of neighbourhood-sized floating communities, each of which would accommodate between 3,500 and 6,500 persons. This unit was estimated to be the minimum size for the economic provision of necessary services. There were two basic neighbourhood modules: one composed of four to six small platforms with housing for about 1,000 people, and the other a larger triangular platform with a capacity of up to 6,500. The larger platforms were expected to weigh somewhere in the region of 75,000 tonnes. Three to six of these neighbourhoods, with a population of 15,000 to 30,000, would form a town. When the community had expanded to the point when it had three to seven towns (90-120,000 persons), it would become a city and extra municipal modules would be added.

Fuller's intention was that, like offshore oil platforms, 'Triton' modules could be serially produced at well-equipped shipyards or dry docks, even if these were at considerable distances from their destinations, and then towed into position. Each module would be completed with factory-made dwelling units installed before delivery. He even proposed land-locked Triton elements called 'Pro-To-City' units as urban modules for his Toronto City Centre renewal project of 1972.

No Triton City was ever built in the United States but, like some other large projects considered by Fuller, the idea attracted great attention in Japan, where an earlier scheme inspired by Shoriki, the proposed 4 kilometre high Yomiuri tower was still under consideration at the time of its publication. Twenty years later projects for artificial and floating islands derived from the Tetrahedronal and Triton City prototypes are already under construction in Japan to house an

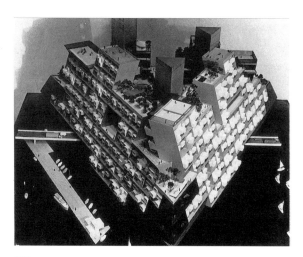

A second marine project on a smaller scale than 'Tetrahedronal City' was the 1968 project 'Triton City' *(below)*. Consisting of interconnected floating accommodation modules with populations of between 3,000 and 6,500 persons, moored adjacent to existing cities *(right)*. This project was financed by the United States Department of Housing and Urban Development but was not proceeded with except in Japan, where the present building of Kansai artificial island *(below, right)* off Osaka owes much to the Triton project.

increasing population and provide offshore services. Originally planned in 1966 as a large tensegrity mast on three legs, Fuller and Sadao's Yomiuri Tower was proposed as a TV station and observation building for a wealthy Japanese corporation. It was intended to equip it with a pressurized observation capsule over 30 storeys tall at its summit to provide a 360 degree view of all the Japanese islands and the Pacific Ocean. Subsequent studies proved that such a tall structure - 200 metres higher than the summit of Mount Fuji - could not have withstood high altitude winds. As a result six supporting cables were added to the supporting legs. These cables were to have been anchored by vast tetrahedral feet with apartment housing complexes built into them, each of which would have been taller than the Eiffel Tower. Office floors built into the central column up to the junction of the supporting legs with the main frame would have been twice as tall as the twin towers of the New York World Trade Centre.

In its second form the Yomiuri project was technically entirely feasible but it was defeated in the end by a final cost estimate of $1.5 billion - six times the projected cost of the earlier version. If it had been erected it would have immediately have become the world's tallest building and would have remained so to this day.

One other major urban renewal project, related in scale to the Harlem towers, was 'Old Man River', a megastructure conceived in 1971 for a black comunity group in East Saint Louis led by the dancer Katherine Dunham. The scheme proposed by Fuller and Sadao was for a gigantic crater-shaped structure on the banks of the Mississipi river. Stretching nearly a kilometre from rim to rim this immense dish was to provide homes for 25,000 families. The provision of a huge geodesic dome above the crater was to provide climate control for all seasons. As with all Fuller's megastructures, 'Old Man River' was to be an integrated settlement with supermarkets, offices, recreational areas and parking included.

'Old Man River' attracted considerable publicity during the early 1970s and some fundraising for the

The last of Fuller and Sadao's building megastructure proposals was 'Old Man River', a 1971 project for a stadium-shaped settlement on the banks of the Mississipi in Saint Louis that would have stretched one kilometre from rim to rim. Climate control was to have been attained by means of a vast transparent covering dome (below) raised above the highest level of the commercial and accomodation structures.

OLD MAN RIVER ...1973
AN UMBRELLAED TOWN CONCEPT
FOR EAST ST. LOUIS, ILLINOIS
R. BUCKMINSTER FULLER

estimated $1 billion cost was attempted. A project office with detailed drawings and models still remained open in 1988. Lack of government financial assistance however makes it extremely unlikely that work will be commenced, let alone completed by the target date of 2004.

Perhaps the most ambitious of all Fuller and Sadao's utopian projects was a scheme that grew out of the 'Dymaxion Air-Ocean World Map' and involved a massive linear engineering project rather than the construction of a significant building. It started in 1969 when Fuller was exploring the possibilities of the 'World Game' that had begun with the Cornell University 'Miniature World' and later spun-off into resource analyses played on large-scale globes and charts. Fuller related what he knew of the history of long distance electricity transmission and suddenly realized that it was perfectly possible to transmit energy across international time zones and thus, in theory, balance out base loads and peak loads by connecting troughs in one time zone to peaks in another. Pursuing this idea Fuller and his New York 'World Game' students drafted out a global high-voltage transmission grid that took in all the continents and all the time zones. As he observed to the film maker Robert Snyder afterwards:

'With this project you could really see for the first time what the Design Science Revolution could mean if it was applied at the right scale. You *could* have a world electricity transmission network and it *would* double effective generating capacity overnight. To heck with the money side - what we wanted was to harness that unused energy and make it work.'

While the 76 metre three-quarter sphere of the United States pavilion at EXPO 67 in Montreal was small compared to Fuller's conception of what might be achieved over Manhattan, it represented the crowning architectural commission of his career. In 1970 Buckminster Fuller and Shoji Sadao were awarded the Gold Medal of the American Institute of Architects in recognition of its achievement. The EXPO 67 dome was also the nearest Fuller ever came to executing any of the giant projects of his later years. Although he was a director of Temcor, his old student Don Richter's Los Angeles company, when the commission for the huge 135 metre aluminium geodesic dome to house the Howard Hughes flying boat 'Spruce Goose' was awarded in 1981, he did not contribute to its design or live to see it completed. Nor did he have any connection with the other famous geodesic structure built after 1967, the Walt Disney 'Spaceship Earth' sphere at EPCOT in Orlando, Florida. This was designed by another of his former students, Peter Floyd, who had worked on the Ford Rotunda as well as the Montreal structure.

At the time of its completion the Montreal three-quarter sphere was the largest geodesic structure in the world and it was immediately recognised as the definitive symbol of the international fair. Furthermore it succeeded in once again placing the enigmatic geometry of the geodesic dome in the forefront of the popular consciousness of advanced technology, at that time subsumed by the United States/Soviet space race that was to end with the triumphant Apollo Moon landing of two years later.

The commission to design the United States pavilion came to Fuller and Sadao three years earlier by way of the director of the World Exposition, a former student of Fuller's at Yale named Jack Masey. While no competition to select the designer was held, Fuller's original proposal was not for a dome at all. Instead it consisted of a vast space frame truss standing on four pylons. The truss was a distant development of the floor system designed sixteen years earlier for the abortive North Carolina automated cotton mill project which was patented in 1961 under the name 'Octet Truss'. Beneath this rectangular platform the exhibition space was to have been suspended without additional ground supports. Visitors would have reached it by way of a single elevator tower containing a battery of lifts. The principal exhibit was to have been an enormous animated 'Dymaxion World Map'.

After some initial design work had been done on this imposing structure it was decided to change the nature of the exhibition and include more diverse material.

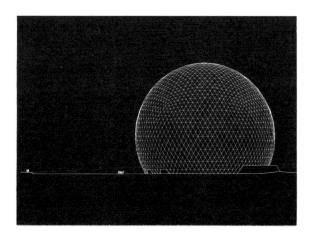

The United States pavilion at EXPO 67 in Montreal was the most prestigious commission Buckminster Fuller executed in his lifetime. Originally designed as an 'octet' truss rectangle, it was later changed to a 76 metre dome, seen as a model at left. The structure itself as made up of steel 'star' tensegrity trusses in the shape of a seven-tenths sphere, enclosed with hexagonal acrylic 'lenses' *(both below)*. Considered the most successful pavilion at the exposition *(right)* it was retained as a permanent structure in the Montreal Expo Park.

167

But the dome unfortunately
caught fire during renovations
in May 1976. The structural
skeleton remains intact today.

All parties involved then agreed that a large dome would provide a better spatial solution. Interestingly the Theme Pavilion at EXPO 70 in Osaka, designed by the Japanese architect and planner Kenzo Tange, took a form remarkably similar to Fuller's abandoned 1967 design.

The dome itself was conceived as a transparent acrylic enclosure with computer controlled 'irises' on each hexagonal lens that followed the course of the sun and provided shade for the interior by actuating filters. The structure was composed of steel 'star' tensegrity trusses descended from the Oregon prototype of eighteen years before. The film maker Robert Snyder wrote of the experience of passing through this harbinger of a future world:

'Inside the dome the walls start going away from you; this has an extraordinary psychological effect of releasing you for suddenly you realize that the walls are not really there... I walked around and listened to what people in the crowd had to say, and they seemed happy in this open but controlled environment. And it was not done according to the aesthetics of architecture as it had been practised up to then. It was done simply in terms of doing the most with the least.'

A final grand thought: twice the height of Frank Lloyd Wright's proposed Mile High Tower, the Yomiuri tower project of 1966 was Fuller and Sadao's first megaproject in Japan. Intended as a television transmitter, office and housing complex and observation tower rising 12,000 metres high, its cable abutments alone would have been taller than the Eiffel Tower. Upwards from the lower bracing point the structure would have been an immense open, tapering tensegrity frame.

ephemeralization and history

'About five years ago I used to work at the Holiday Inn at 36th and Chestnut. I was working there at night and going to nursing school during the day. Most of the waiters and waitresses tended to avoid old people because they're not usually good tippers. But this little old man particularly... I don't know what it was about him that attracted me. For one thing, I thought he looked lonely. I must have waited on him at least eight times while I worked there. He'd always order tea with lemon, and sometimes he's ask for sherbet too. I never knew his full name. He just said 'Call me Bucky' and that was what I called him. He gave me this little card that said 'Cable address Bucky'... He used to make these little drawings for me on ordinary notepad paper. And he'd sign them 'Bucky' and write the date too. He once told me 'Hold on to these, you never know, they might be worth something someday'.'

The Buckminster Fuller Institute Newsletter, October 1983

Recognition was a problem Buckminster Fuller faced all his life. Sometimes he called himself a machinist, sometimes an engineer, sometimes a sailor, sometimes grandiosely an astronaut from Spaceship Earth, sometimes simply a 'trim-tab', after the tiny adjustable control surface that can swing a rudder or an elevator and thus change the direction of a mighty ship or aeroplane.

Recognition is part of a larger problem too. It is part of the crisis of identity of transitory lives in a mass society on a densely populated planet, and part of the crisis of identity of transitory designed objects in a massively duplicating and continuously evolving technology.

The significance of the passage of time and the redundancy of people and things was printed right through Buckminster Fuller's world view. It extended from his interest in the ancient art of rhetoric - through which pre-industrial men had come to understood that the minimum number of words and gestures achieved the maximum effect - to his concern with the engineering challenge of designing the most with the least in a world of indiscriminate production. These apparently disparate matters, and the connections that he saw between them, were part of his most important theory - the theory of ephemeralization.

Unlike the early masterpieces of his architect contemporaries Frank Lloyd Wright, Le Corbusier, Mies van der Rohe and others, Buckminster Fuller's designs - the Dymaxion house, the Dymaxion Deployment Unit, the Wichita house, the geodesic and tensegrity domes, and the giant projects of the 1960s - were all steps towards the ephemeralization, or rendering insignificant, of the problem of shelter, rather than works of architecture. In this sense they were simply tools, but in another sense they transcended the timescale of mere usefulness and attained another scale of value altogether. Today they are in a literal sense anachronisms - timeless achievements in an age of continuous technical development that ruthlessly gives a shelf-life to even its finest manufactures.

This 'shelf-life' is the product of a general acceptance that industrial civilization really is endless. That because scientific and technical development is continuous, no single invention can dawdle in the limelight, but must vacate it swiftly in favour of something cheaper and better, or become part of another composite element

Buckminster Fuller, the philosopher of industrialization - in the form of the bust by Isamu Noguchi.

in a general process of synergetic fusion into a greater whole.

It was Richard Buckminster Fuller who originated the concept of cumulative technical advantage that is called synergy, and he too who gave the whole evolutionary process of which it is a part the name of 'Ephemeralization', from the Greek *ephemeros* meaning 'lasting only a day'. For him the idea that the intractable limitations of nature would yield, one by one, to the power of the human mind, explained and justified the transformation of the 18th century craftsman's priceless timepiece into the 20th century's mass produced quartz watch - a device that is not only infinitely smaller, lighter and more accurate than its hand-made predecessor, but is also just as priceless - in the sense that it has become so universally available as to be almost without value.

For Fuller the watch; the pen; the telephone; the calculator; the camera; the bicycle; electric power; water supply; artificial heat and cold; transport and shelter were all goods or services ephemeralized or destined for ephemeralization. He saw all of them and thousands more as once untamed elements, dangerous or inadequate aspects of the human environment, that were by patient design science slowly being merged into mankind-serving cycles of reproduction and decay like the carbon cycle of living things. He believed that all the deficiencies of human society and all the dangers it feared, could be overcome, resolved and miniaturized into a vast and seamless man-made service technology: a second, organized surface of the earth.

Before he died Fuller saw this grand process of ephemeralization coming true before his eyes. From small indicators he drew large conclusions. Today there is no car without a clock; so telling the time is no longer an appropriate function for a single mechanism, but a subordinate function of almost any enclosure, including a car. Soon there will be no car, no train and no aeroplane without a telephone so long-distance communication too will cease to command its own enclosure - the absurd anachronism of the telephone box - and become instead another subsidiary function of all modes of transport. Today there is no building without water and electric power; soon there will be no buildings without automatic climate control. By then the term 'comfort' will have become an unconsidered adjunct to 'insideness', perhaps eventually to encompass the entire distinction between 'insideness' and 'outsideness' including the availability of information and communication. In a subliminal return to the mid-20th century train of thought that led Buckminster Fuller to the geodesic dome itself, the component parts of this 'comfort' will not even be called buildings.

One of the things that this theory of ephemeralization shows us is how to approach the serious purpose of design, as opposed to the triviality of mere styling, in the context of human survival. In Buckminster Fuller's formulation of the need for a 'Design Science' we can see how, amid a cascade of innovations that diffuse and coalesce with bewildering speed, there can still be individual feats of design that can become

The chaotic urban world of the 20th century as portrayed by Fuller.

175

metaphorical objects of pilgrimage, even if they are never made or built. As the Dymaxion house, the Dymaxion Deployment Unit and the dome over Manhattan demonstrate, it is by truly extraordinary feats of ephemeralizing design - not by tricks of fashion or the luck of production success - that evolving complexes of environmental technology achieve recognition and survive in human consciousness.

Design work that conforms to the long term multifold trend towards ephemeralization retains its identity because it fits into a recognizable framework, a pattern of mankind-bettering technological advance, instead of an endless spiral of shocks and sensations. Fuller's works in this genre have already become mythological because recognition of their separate identity is necessary if we are to continue to be able to believe in order working itself out - as opposed to chaos closing in. In a phrase the design achievements that are the building blocks of ephemeralization are landmarks on the map of synergy; and without such landmarks to direct product evolution, design dissolves into the abstract powerlessness of art.

Art history finds it difficult to deal with a design like the Dymaxion house, which never really existed but is nonetheless a landmark in technological evolution. Art history cannot grant it the status of 'timelessness' that it freely awards to the great artistic and architectural achievements of the past - which are worshipped as objects of value irrespective of their usefulness (or lack of it) or their relevance (or lack of it) to present ways and means. A complex design process that produces a simple product-idea, like a factory-built home, is not art because it belongs to another kind of history.

The same impasse is presented even if the objects that emerge are real. A physical product like the 'Wichita' house of 1946, or its contemporary, the British AIROH aluminium prefabricated house: a pioneering car like Vittorio Jano's independent suspension, front wheel drive 1937 Lancia Aprilia; or even a 75 year-old aeroplane design like the corrugated duralumin Junkers D-1, the first all-metal monocoque cantilever monoplane - all these objects displayed the first and best resolution of so many functional demands and creative insights that, although they are not 'art', they remain alive in the minds of designers long after they have ceased to be new. Art history or no art history, under the rules of ephemeralization they will retain 'classic' status until the concept 'building', the concept 'automobile' or the concept 'aeroplane' cease to possess any useful meaning.

To a degree the steel frame buildings of Mies van der Rohe, the Usonian houses of Frank Lloyd Wright and the concrete villas of Le Corbusier possess this unique combination of rich invention and technical completeness that is immune to the vagaries of fashion. No student of the evolution of the modern house can ignore the Farnsworth house, Falling Water or the Maison Savoye, for these three works of architecture too embody formal and structural relationships that are not the ordinary outcome of fashion or the display of wealth. They too stem from the exercise of a creative genius. But they have a crippling weakness that their creators can no longer do anything about. It is a weakness that is in the eye of the beholder, because our way of looking at them has been chained to the classificatory system of art history.

The art historical system perpetually endeavours to lever invention away from the restlessly evolving vocabulary of art and science in the service of man - the language that Buckminster Fuller spoke - back into the passive world of scarcity and value judgement that he correctly identified as the greatest enemy of human success. We should be in no doubt that the incompatibility of these two world views is absolute. We need only consider a simple example: the contrast between Fuller's 1940 adaptation of thousands of standard steel grain bins into a globally-distributable emergency housing system - and the proposal by architect Bruce Goff a decade later to use four of the same grain bins as bedrooms in a private house for a wealthy client.

The distinction between these two value systems illuminates the convention that has grown up in the history of Modern Architecture that Buckminster

Fuller's '4-D' and 'Dymaxion' projects, his domes and his megastructures as somehow outside the main line of serious development, almost an irrelevance to it.

That there is a 'main line' of Modern development in historical terms is indisputable, even if we ignore the dubious claims of some alleged 19th century antecedents. No historian would argue against the existence of a palpable progression from Adolf Loos's Steiner House of 1910 to, say, Moshe Safdie's 1967 'Habitat'. Into this Modern bloodstock line we would expect, if only through their dates and the publicity that surrounded them, Buckminster Fuller's projects to find their place. But they do not.

Consider the case of the 1929 Dymaxion house model, based on drawings made three years before Le Corbusier's *Les Heures Claires* and nine years before Frank Lloyd Wright's 'Falling Water'. Photographs of it have been published regularly since 1932, yet still

The first two stepping stones on the path to ephemeralization. First the Dymaxion World Map *(below)*, seeing the world in a new geometry, patented in 1946. Second the 1952 chart of the 20th century, and graphic proof that 'design science' can extract more from less and make the majority of the world's population 'haves' instead of 'have nots' *(right)*.

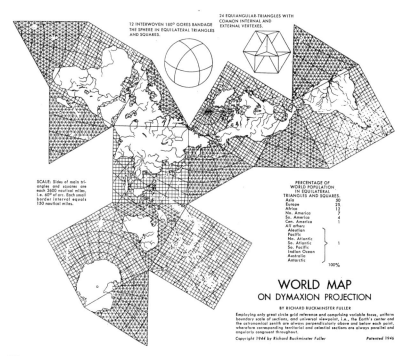

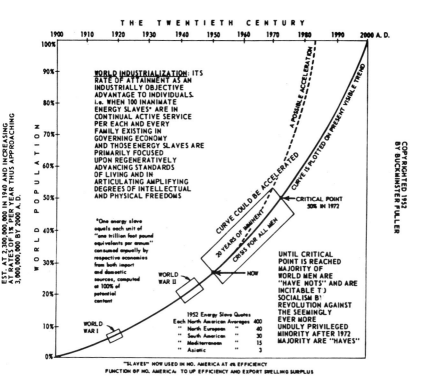

WORLD INDUSTRIALIZATION: ITS RATE OF ATTAINMENT AS AN INDUSTRIALLY OBJECTIVE ADVANTAGE TO INDIVIDUALS. i.e. WHEN 100 INANIMATE ENERGY SLAVES* ARE IN CONTINUAL ACTIVE SERVICE PER EACH AND EVERY FAMILY EXISTING IN GOVERNING ECONOMY AND THOSE ENERGY SLAVES ARE PRIMARILY FOCUSED UPON REGENERATIVELY ADVANCING STANDARDS OF LIVING AND IN ARTICULATING AMPLIFYING DEGREES OF INTELLECTUAL AND PHYSICAL FREEDOMS

*One energy slave equals each unit of "one trillion foot pound equivalents per annum" consumed annually by respective economies from both import and domestic sources, computed at 100% of potential content

WORLD POPULATION

EST. AT 2,300,000,000 IN 1940 AND INCREASING AT RATES OF 1% PER YEAR THUS APPROACHING 3,000,000,000 BY 2000 A.D.

COPYRIGHTED 1952 BY BUCKMINSTER FULLER

A POSSIBLE ACCELERATION

CURVE IS PLOTTED ON PRESENT VISIBLE TREND

CURVE COULD BE ACCELERATED

20 YEARS OF IMMINENT CRISIS FOR ALL MEN

CRITICAL POINT 50% IN 1972

NOW

WORLD WAR II

WORLD WAR I

UNTIL CRITICAL POINT IS REACHED MAJORITY OF WORLD MEN ARE "HAVE NOTS" AND ARE INCITABLE TO SOCIALISM BY REVOLUTION AGAINST THE SEEMINGLY EVER MORE UNDULY PRIVILEGED MINORITY AFTER 1972 MAJORITY ARE "HAVES"

1952 Energy Slave Quotas
Each North American Averages 400
" North European " 40
" South American " 30
" Mediterranean " 15
" Asiatic " 3

"SLAVES" NOW USED IN NO. AMERICA AT 4% EFFICIENCY
FUNCTION OF NO. AMERICA TO UP EFFICIENCY AND EXPORT SWELLING SURPLUS

it does not slot as easily into the history of Modern Architecture as it should. So much so that despite being published regularly in the lay and business press, none of the principal historians who wrote contemporaneously with the ascendancy of the Modern Movement even mentions it - nor any of the images of Dymaxion dwelling units, single or multi-storey, that emerged during Fuller's first period of public notice.

Niklaus Pevsner does not mention Buckminster Fuller at all. Nor does James Richards. Henry Russell Hitchcock and Philip Johnson do not mention Fuller. Writing two decades later, Vincent Scully mentions only the geodesic dome, remarking disparagingly; 'it can only do one thing and make one shape'. And writing later still William Curtis make an equally dismissive bow in a footnote; 'the Dymaxion house as an aesthetic arrangement... was scarcely inspiring'. Contemporaneously with Curtis, Kenneth Frampton acknowledges the significance of *Shelter* magazine and does set Fuller aside as a 'rugged pioneering individualist', but a less enthusiastic assessment is to follow. Fuller becomes 'utilitarian yet complacent' and before long he is reduced to the status of a *Mechanix Illustrated* do-it-yourselfer, good with blowtorch but untroubled by intellectual hoo-ha.

The only noble exception among art historians is Reyner Banham. In 1960, in *Theory and Design in the First Machine Age*, Banham does experimentally project Fuller into his rightful place as the most farsighted of all the modern functionalists of the pioneering generation. But, looked at closely, Banham's enthusiasm is only half-hearted. He clearly knows little of Fuller's early years and carefully confines him to a passage or two in the last chapter of his book. Worse still, the quotation that he provides to substantiate Fuller's early dismissal of Bauhaus Modernism was actually written 28 years later than he claims. But despite these limitations, Banham does see that the pioneers of Modernism and Buckminster Fuller correct two different value systems. If the theory of 'ephemeralization' is represent, then 'functionalism' is at best a small part of it, not an alternative theory.

Because of his transcending theoretical position, Buckminster Fuller did not follow the same rules of technology and image transfer as Le Corbusier, Walter Gropius and Mies van der Rohe. Blessed as he was with wartime experience in the US Navy and years as a building material producer, in both of which fields he had been required to familiarize himself with the most advanced technology extant, Fuller possessed a far more impressive technical background than the society of millionaires and art collectors gave to the noncombatant Le Corbusier; or a commission in a cavalry regiment during the Great War awarded Walter Gropius; or even the humble duty of guarding railway lines in the same conflict gave to the private soldier Ludwig Mies. For Fuller the Navy was not a technical world evolving towards 'pure types', but a prototype maelstrom of restless and endless change. It was constantly moving; 'from the wire to the wireless, the track

Thirdly there is the 1964 chart of the industrial revolution showing the exponential increase in the rate of discovery of elements.

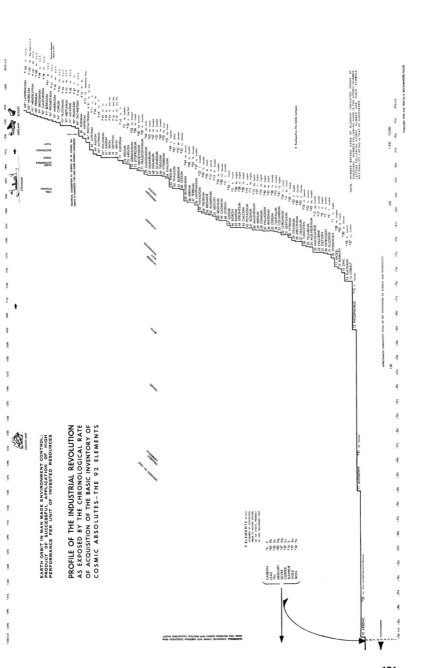

PROFILE OF THE INDUSTRIAL REVOLUTION
AS EXPOSED BY THE CHRONOLOGICAL RATE
OF ACQUISITION OF THE BASIC INVENTORY OF
COSMIC ABSOLUTES—THE 92 ELEMENTS

EARTH ORBIT IN MAN MADE ENVIRONMENT CONTROL:
PRODUCT OF SUCCESSFUL APPLICATION OF HIGH
PERFORMANCE PER UNIT OF INVESTED RESOURCES

to the trackless, the visible to the invisible, where more and more could be done with less and less'. Above all it was a practical world in which responding to innovation was a routine procedure, not an exciting event indulged from time to time for its intellectual *frisson*.

When, a decade after he left the Navy for the last time, Fuller explained in the pages of *Shelter* the origins of the Dymaxion house in the cantilevered wooden lighthouses of the coast of Maine, and the source of the Dymaxion Deployment Unit and the Wichita House in the production-model gas holders and grain bins of pre-war America, he was not post-rationalizing a photographic resemblance in order to create an art historical past for himself. Nor was the relationship between the power pylons that he illustrated, and the subsequent development of the geodesic dome and its related space frames, an aesthetic analogy, like Le Corbusier's aping of interplane struts in the form of *pilotis*.

Fuller knew that all the standard products he illustrated were made using techniques that had been arrived at by breaking seemingly insuperable fabrication tasks down into manageable man and machine jobs. Proceeding practically he first found out what those tasks were so that he could understand how things were put together - over the years this contributed to a vast mental and physical library of curiosities (the 'Chronofile') that was his greatest resource - and only later when the practicalities had been filed away did he make his '4-D' contribution, which was to propose that something else, more useful to humanity than the first product, might be put together in the same way. The most perfect illustration of this whole methodology, indeed a transformation that embodies the essence of what wonders can be achieved by the simplest technology transfer, is again the conversion of the standard Butler grain store - which was already mass-produced - into the far more necessary prefabricated house which at the time was not.

The art historians who still rule our perception of architecture and design, men and women who quickly came to terms with the process of *image* transfer that led Amedee Ozenfant and Charles-Edouard Jeanneret to design reinforced concrete buildings that *looked like* the white-painted steel superstructures of ocean liners standing on the tapered interplane struts of biplane aircraft, have never made an analogous effort to understand the pure technology transfer of Fuller's work. Was this because Fuller consistently and unrestrainedly abused them, as we have seen. Or was there another reason? It cannot have been because Fuller was a dreamer who actually built very little, for this is neither fair nor true. The Italian Futurists Sant 'Elia and Chiattone, like the Russian Constructivist Leonidov, built nothing at all, yet their names are found in even the most cursory histories of Modern architecture. In any case, although historians apparently refuse to recognize what contemporary practitioners dismissed as 'peas-in-a-pod designs', the architect of the Dymaxion House did actually build more buildings than Le Corbusier, Walter Gropius and Mies van der Rohe.

There were only three Dymaxion cars ever built, of which one survives, and only two Wichita Houses, later clumsily combined into the single survivor; but between 1923 and 1927, 240 buildings were erected using the 'Stockade' compressed wood-shavings block system, and the production of the blocks for these buildings was carried out on machines that Fuller designed. Fifteen years later, according to John McHale, the rate of production of Fuller's 'Dymaxion Deployment Units' reached 1,000 a day before strategic reallocations of steel terminated it. And finally no less than 300,000 geodesic domes based on Fuller's patents were erected between 1954 and his death in 1983.

In the end we come by a process of elimination to what must be the real reason for Buckminster Fuller's anomalous position in the history of Modern Architecture: the paucity and weakness of his early writings. Unlike Le Corbusier, whose early career was immensely aided by the publication of two important and widely translated books - Amedee Ozenfant's *Foundations of Modern Art* and his own *Towards a New Architecture* - Buckminster Fuller was hampered by a lack of accessible publications, an absence of convincing imagery, and by his own impenetrable writing style.

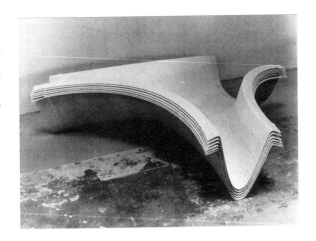

Three exercises in ephemeralization. The 'Monohex' or 'Fly's Eye' dome *(left & right)*, first patented in 1965 as a method of reducing the structural weight - and thus the cost - of a simple dwelling to the lowest possible level. Fuller developed it in various materials including steel, aluminium, and glass fibre until 1978. Constructed from a single-shape component this represented the last and simplest of all Fuller's approaches to mass-production low-cost housing.

The tubular catamaran rowing shell *(left)* that Fuller designed in 1947 shows the same development. Each bow and stern end is socket-assembled in lengths of light aluminium tube. The oarsman sits in a light plastic nacelle and the width can be adjusted to suit. Unique advantage of catamaran form is stability. Lone oarsman can climb back aboard unaided.

Where Le Corbusier's writings - and above all Ozenfant's illustrations - made the derivations and principles of the New European Architecture crystal clear from 1921 onwards, at first in magazine articles in *L'Esprit Nouveau*, and later in books and actual buildings, Fuller's early work is confusingly under-recorded. In his case the national newspaper press cuttings and interviews exist, and have been tirelessly republished, but the convincing images in professional magazines do not begin until 1932 and the seminal book, or manifesto, despite many efforts, does not appear until a determined co-writer, Robert Marks, forces it through far too late in 1960.

'4-D', chronologically Fuller's equivalent to *Towards a New Architecture*, the work of which Anne Hewlett Fuller sketched him completing the manuscript, was 'published' in Chicago in 1928 - in a hand bound 'edition' of 200 copies - virtually all of which were, as we have seen, wasted (for historical purposes) on friends, relatives and prominent people. '4-D' was not destined to be printed again until 1970 - by which time *Towards a New Architecture* had been reprinted eleven times in its English translation alone. Even when '4D Timelock', as '4-D' was retitled, finally did appear, it was not only altered and provided with new illustrations, but humiliatingly prefaced by its New Mexico publishers with the warning; 'Today some of the book makes sense and some of it doesn't make sense.'

Worse still, the same uncertainty ultimately surrounds what is generally described as Fuller's own magazine, the Philadelphia published *Shelter* (formerly *T-Square Club Journal* and *T-Square*), which appeared under one title or another in 1931 and 1932. The 'clean-up' design for the Dymaxion house - the design always illustrated today - was first published in a professional architectural magazine in March 1932 in *Architectural Forum*, and only subsequently in *Shelter*. If, as we have noted, Fuller and his biographers, even the most recent, Lloyd Steven Sieden, claim that he owned and published *Shelter* himself and that it made a profit - without advertising - on a circulation of 2,500 and a cover price of $2.00, why did he not publish his own design himself? Perhaps the answer to this question is to be found in the surviving copies of *Shelter* (May to November 1932), where the editor is cited as Maxwell Levinson; the Associate Editor as the architect George Howe (of Howe and Lescaze), and the Managing Editor as Leon Levinson.

Another fundamental question about *Shelter* magazine concerns the authorship of its articles. The same surviving copies show that most though not all of them are unsigned, and although these include many, like the important 'Streamlining', that were very probably written by Fuller, there is no incontrovertible proof that they were his work alone. This very un-European indifference to authorship and bibliographical exactitude makes it particularly difficult to use the ideas and images attributed to Fuller in *Shelter* magazine as tools to rewrite the history of Modern Architecture and challenge its dominant value system.

There remains the text of Fuller's book *Nine Chains*

to the Moon, published by a reputable publisher, Lipincott of Philadelphia and New York in 1938. *Nine Chains* is a book that even at that late stage might have been Fuller's seminal work. Like '*4-D*' however it is virtually unillustrated - certainly its child's sketches of 'BOZAR' versus 'MODUN' houses cannot be considered influential images - and it is still convolutedly difficult to read. Indeed where the *Shelter* articles generally attributed to Fuller show the pedigree of his ideas with startling clarity, the 1938 book that should have assembled and codified them, only buries them once again in that abstruse geopolitical knowingness that clouded his earlier writings.

There is a further problem with *Nine Chains to the Moon* that, like the transformation from '*4-D*' to '*4-D Timelock*', concerns authenticity. At its first publication *Nine Chains to the Moon* was endorsed by Albert Einstein, who also endorsed Le Corbusier's *Le Modulor* a few years later, but its sales were minimal. It was out of print from 1939 until the University of Southern Illinois, followed by Doubleday, reissued it in the wake of the successful 1960 publication of Robert Marks' *The Dymaxion World of Buckminster Fuller*. This second edition was abridged by 60 pages, including the removal of all appendices and charts. Furthermore an important list of 22 events or inventions that Fuller had said were certain to come about 'between July 12th 1938 and July 12th 1948' was dispensed with, presumably because so few of them had happened, even by July 12th 1963 when the book was reprinted. Since one of the discarded predictions was 'The main system of general education instruction to go on the air and screen'; another was the 'Inception of the completely mechanized stock exchange and world-wide repeater-linked popular employment thereof'; and a third was the 'evolutionary abolition of the terms 'unemployed' and 'on relief' and the substitution therefor of 'Social Reserve' and 'Industrial Reserve'', these excisions were certainly ill-advised. The fact that they were made without notice in the reprint is doubly disturbing.

One way or another this tradition of lost opportunity in Fuller's writings was to persist for the rest of

his life, even though he eventually became so famous that his books commanded large advances and sold well whether they could be understood by their readers or not. More than 30 years after the publication of *Nine Chains to the Moon*, his massive tome *Synergetics*, published after seven years of work by a dedicated collaborator and editor, Edward Applewhite, has no index and is virtually unreadable as narrative - the latter a state of affairs barely remedied by its rapidly produced sequel *Synergetics II*, which incorporates an index to both volumes. *Critical Path* too, which was published in 1981, his last major book before his death, suffers from this same weakness. Though narrative rather than mathematical, it is jaggedly discursive and consists largely of transcribed lectures and ghost writing by Kiyoshi Kuromiya that wanders back and forth through some of the same themes as *Nine Chains* at a distance of fifty years. Like all Fuller's books, its length too is bulked out by an unnecessarily detailed and Quixotic chronology of world historical events placing the inventor's actions in a cosmic context.

In the end it is perhaps in the nature of the creative life of Richard Buckminster Fuller that the search for an unadulterated early text should be fruitless. Designing machine-made objects that have become part of the alphabet of technological ephemeralization is a rare accomplishment; as rare as the life of an individual whose creative energies did not wane with age, the corruption of failure, or the distractions of success. And yet, alongside the role of the unnamed women Fuller described to Anwar Dil, we must remember the role of the other phantom collaborators, the names of so many of whom have vanished into the penumbra surrounding his own shining reputation.

The creative life of Buckminster Fuller was such a tremendous unfolding of applied intellectual energy that it is and must remain primarily a visual and aural legacy, best absorbed through the contemporary media of film, video, photography, tape recording, transcription and recollection. In this as in so many other ways, Fuller shows us that he really was a citizen of the future. For behind the art historical neglect, the confusion of dates and the uncertainty of collaboration that dog his achievements, lies his triumphant refusal, even after death, to be confined to a wheelchair as yet another 20th century intellectual artefact.

bibliography

Emily and Per Ola d'Aulaire. 'The Man Who Saw Tomorrow'. *Reader's Digest*, February 1985

Reyner Banham. Theory and Design in the First Machine Age. London 1960

David Boyd. *Technocracy and Modern Architecture.* USC Yearbook 1978-79. Los Angeles 1979

R. Buckminster Fuller and Anwar Dil. *Humans in Universe.* Mouton, New York 1983

R. Buckminster Fuller. 'Experimental Probing of Architectural Initiative'. *RIBA Journal.* London, October 1958

Buckminster Fuller Institute. *Synergetic Stew: explorations in Dymaxion dining.* (Introduction by R. Buckminster Fuller). Buckminster Fuller Institute, Philadelphia 1982 *Buckminster Fuller: an autobiographical monologue/scenario.* Documented and edited Robert Snyder. St Martin's Press, New York 1980

The Buckminster Fuller Reader. (Ed. James Meller) Jonathan Cape, London 1970

'R. Buckminster Fuller Retrospective'. (Ed. Michael Ben-Eli). *Architectural Design*, London, December 1972

R. Buckminster Fuller. *Basic Biography.* Buckminster Fuller Institute, Los Angeles 1983

R. Buckminster Fuller and Kiyoshi Kuromiya. *Critical Path*. Hutchinson, London 1983

R. Buckminster Fuller and Robert Marks. *The Dymaxion World of Buckminster Fuller*. Southern Illinois University Press, Carbondale 1960

R. Buckminster Fuller. *Inventions: the patented works of R. Buckminster Fuller*. St Martin's Press. New York 1983

R. Buckminster Fuller. *Nine Chains to the Moon*. Lippincott, Philadelphia and New York 1938. Abridged edition, University of Southern Illinois, Carbondale 1963. Reprinted, Doubleday Anchor, New York 1971.

R. Buckminster Fuller. *No More Secondhand God and other writings*. Southern Illinois University Press. Carbondale 1963

R. Buckminster Fuller. *Operating Manual for Spaceship Earth*. E.P, Dutton. New York 1978

R. Buckminster Fuller. *Sketchbook*. University City Science Centre, Philadelphia 1981.

R. Buckminster Fuller. *4-D Timelock*. Biotechnic Press. Albuquerque 1972.

R. Buckminster Fuller. *50 Years of the Design Science Revoluion and the World Game*. World Resources Inventory, Philadelphia 1969.

'Richard Buckminster Fuller'. (Ed. John McHale). *Architectural Design*, London, July 1961

William J.R. Curtis. *Modern Architecture since 1900*. Oxford 1982.

Kenneth Frampton. *Modern Architecture: a critical history*. London 1980

Mary Emma Harris. *The Arts at Black Mountain College*. MIT Press. Cambridge 1987.

Henry Russell Hitchcock and Philip Johnson. *The International Style: architecture since 1922*. New York 1932 (reprinted 1966).

Morton Keller (Ed). *The New Deal: what was it?* Holt, Rinehart and Winston, New York 1963

Z. S. Makowski. 'A Survey of Recent Three-dimensional Structures'. *Architectural Design*, London, January 1966

John McHale. *R. Buckminster Fuller*. Prentice Hall International, London 1962.

Niklaus Pevsner. *Pioneers of Modern Design from William Morris to Walter Gropius*. London 1936

J. M. Richards. *The Functional Tradition*. London 1958

Vincent Scully. *American Architecture and Urbanism*. New York 1969.

'Concealed Plumbing', 'Streamlining', 'Journal of the Space Hotel' and 'Olympic Village Notes' (all unsigned). *Shelter* magazine, Philadelphia. November 1932.

Lloyd Steven Sieden. *Buckminster Fuller's Universe: an appreciation*. Plenum Press. New York 1989.

Calvin Tomkins. 'In the Outlaw Area'. *The New Yorker*, 8th January 1966

'Universal Requirements Checklist: Buckminster Fuller'. (Ed. John McHale). *Architectural Design*, London, March 1960

James Ward (Ed). *The Artifacts of R. Buckminster Fuller* (Vols I-IV). Garland Publishing, New York 1985.